Edgeworth and the Development of Neoclassical Economics

Edgeworth and the Development of Neoclassical Economics

JOHN CREEDY

Basil Blackwell

First published 1986

Basil Blackwell Ltd
108 Cowley Road, Oxford OX4 1JF, UK

Basil Blackwell Inc.
432 Park Avenue South, Suite 1505,
New York, NY 10016, USA

British Library Cataloguing in Publication Data
Creedy, John, 1949–
Edgeworth and the development of neoclassical economics.
1. Edgeworth, Francis Ysidro
I. Title
330′.092′4 HB103.E3
ISBN 0-631-14923-6

Library of Congress Cataloging in Publication Data
Creedy, John, 1949–
Edgeworth and the development of neoclassical economics.
Bibliography: p.
Includes index.
1. Neoclassical school of economics. 2. Edgeworth, Francis Ysidro, 1845–1926. I. Title.
HB98.2.C74 1986 330.15′5 85-26750
ISBN 0-631-14923-6

Phototypeset by Dobbie Typesetting Service, Plymouth, Devon
Printed in Great Britain by Page Bros (Norwich), Ltd

Contents

Acknowledgements

It is a pleasure to thank Professor Denis O'Brien for his considerable help during the preparation of this book. I have benefited from extensive comments on earlier papers and drafts of each chapter, and it is no exaggeration to say that the book would not have been written without his encouragement. However, he cannot be held responsible for any shortcomings which remain; indeed, I am fully conscious of my failure to attain the standard exemplified in his own writings on the history of economic thought. I have also benefited from numerous constructive comments on an earlier draft by Roger Backhouse, which have (I hope) led to improvements in the text. I am very grateful to Professor Mark Casson for advice regarding publication. This was extremely valuable at a time when most publishers seemed to take the view that virtually no one would wish to read anything about the work of (someone who was in their view) an obscure economist like Edgeworth. I therefore appreciate very much the interest shown by René Olivieri of Basil Blackwell. I am also grateful to Professor R. D. C. Black and Mrs Christina Colvin for answering queries regarding Jevons and the Edgeworth family, respectively. Oliver Dickinson of Durham University kindly provided translations of the numerous pieces of Greek and Latin which appear in *Mathematical Psychics*. Finally, I should like to thank Kathryn Cowton for her superb typing, and her infinite patience in the face of my propensity to make alterations to the text.

ACKNOWLEDGEMENTS

Introduction

Virtually every student of economics has probably heard of Edgeworth, if only from learning about the 'Edgeworth box', still one of the most widely used analytical devices in the subject. A smaller number may have seen passing references to his analyses of duopoly, his discussion of progressive income taxation, and some may perhaps have read of his comments on the theory of optimal tariffs. More advanced students interested in general equilibrium analysis will be familiar with the rather inappropriately named 'Edgeworth's conjecture': the idea that the 'recontracting process' of barter leads to the unique price-taking equilibrium so long as there is a sufficiently large number of traders. Students with a special interest in the history of economic analysis will probably know of Edgeworth's contribution to the Royal Economic Society, as first editor of the *Economic Journal*. They will also perhaps appreciate that, as Drummond Professor of Political Economy at Oxford, Edgeworth was acknowledged as one of the leading economists of his generation, with a wide range of international contacts. References to his important contributions to the theory of index numbers and to mathematical statistics will perhaps also be familiar.

In general histories of economic thought very little attention is, however, usually given to Edgeworth (with the important exception of Hutchison, 1953). Edgeworth, like most of the economists of his generation, was overshadowed by Alfred Marshall, and indeed Edgeworth was quite content to remain in the penumbra of the leading authority. As Schumpeter has stressed about the period from 1870 to 1914, 'In England, the period is emphatically the Marshallian Age. His success was as great as [Adam] Smith's' (1954, p. 83). Keynes's biographical sketch (1972) is probably still the most widely read source of information about Edgeworth's life and work although it was written well over half a century ago. It is most unlikely that very many people now read Edgeworth's work in the original. This consists of three rather inaccessible early monographs and many specialist articles and reviews, the most important of which are collected in his three volumes of *Papers Relating to Political Economy* (1925). All of his work was addressed to his professional colleagues in a terse, uncompromising and highly individual style.

A strongly prevalent attitude seems to be that Edgeworth was a rather idiosyncratic person, whose papers are highly allusive, very difficult to read and usually concerned with criticism or with minor points of highly abstract theory. The comforting judgement is usually made that Edgeworth's works were so steeped in an old-fashioned brand of utilitarianism that they can be safely ignored now that modern economics has dispensed with such outmoded cardinalist fallacies. However, a closer analysis shows that although Edgeworth was indeed exceptional in his range and depth of knowledge and in his originality, he was in many ways a good representative of a significant group of late Victorian intellectuals. His works are without doubt very difficult to follow, but his preoccupations and values were certainly shared by many of his contemporaries. In this connection it is interesting to read Viner's judgement, written early in the Second World War, that, 'Marshall's economics is now distinctly that of a generation which is past, and is increasingly *not* that of our own . . . Both the Victorian complacency with respect to the present and the Victorian optimism with respect to future progress are now utterly inappropriate' (1958, p. 261).

Although Edgeworth's work has received relatively little serious attention from historians of economic thought, care must be taken not to exaggerate this point. The three economists most closely associated with the so-called 'marginal revolution', Jevons (d. 1882), Walras (d. 1910) and Menger (d. 1921), have of course been examined extensively. But the next 'generation' of economists, whose working lives overlapped significantly with the above trio, have yet to be examined really seriously. The nature of their contribution to economics is not so well understood as that of the early 'neoclassicals', and certainly not well understood in comparison with that of the classical economists. It is worth mentioning that many of the group of neoclassical economists, who may be termed 'late Victorians', died within a few years of each other. These include, for example, Böhm-Bawerk (d. 1914), Pareto (d. 1923), Marshall (d. 1924), Pantaleoni (d. 1924), Edgeworth (d. 1926), Wicksell (d. 1926), Wieser (d. 1926), and Wicksteed (d. 1928). Others may easily be added to this list, such as Barone (d. 1924), Launhardt (d. 1918), and J. S. Nicholson (d. 1927).

This group took an important part in the professionalization of the subject during the later years of the nineteenth century, and nearly all its members became professors of economics although their early careers were not in economics. During the 1930s, and especially after the Second World War, the character both of economists and of the way in which economics was studied changed somewhat. The background and the range of interests of professional economists became much narrower, and unfortunately economists became much more insular. The narrow training received by modern economists makes it difficult to approach the work of the late Victorians with a sympathetic appreciation of their major preoccupations, although superficially there may seem to be many similarities. A great deal of groundwork needs to be done before their work can be fully appreciated; for example, there is still no full length study of Marshall, for whom the secondary literature is so much larger than the others in the group.

The purpose of the present study is to examine Edgeworth's main contribution to economics. Because of his originality and his position of authority, an understanding of Edgeworth's contribution helps to shed some light on the wider development of neoclassical economics. Some comment is necessary in view of the complaint made by Viner that, 'the lack of interest of English economists in the history of the ideas which they manipulate is notorious', and especially his following comment that 'when they do embark upon ventures in doctrinal history, it is generally to exalt a hero' (1958, p. 396). This book has certainly not been written to 'exalt a hero'; indeed any reader of Edgeworth will rapidly realize that he does not have hero potential, and of course in his own lifetime he had no close followers. This book really represents at most only a very small contribution to a wider research programme. However, it is hoped that the book will be of interest not only to those with a special interest in the history of economic analysis, but also to economists who use and develop the results of this leading neoclassical economist and wish to see those results in perspective. No attempt has been made to discuss his significant contributions to mathematical statistics, nor indeed to provide a comprehensive analysis of his economic writing. This would not be possible within such a short compass.

It has been very difficult to decide precisely how much background detail should be provided in order to avoid the complaint by one group that there is insufficient historical material, and by another group that there is insufficient theoretical detail. With the inevitable need for compromise there is an obvious danger of 'falling between two stools'. However, mathematics have been reduced to a minimum, and an attempt has been made to prevent the text from becoming too cluttered with references and notes; all notes on further reading have been placed in separate sections at the end of each chapter.

Very few personal details are available about Edgeworth's life, and no attempt has been made here to provide a biography or 'portrait'. Chapter 1 provides some brief details of his career and family background, along with a discussion of his approach to economics. However, Edgeworth did not begin to publish in economics until he was over thirty years old. For this reason it is instructive to examine closely Edgeworth's transition from (among other subjects) moral philosophy, treated mathematically, to economics. Without this background it is not possible fully to appreciate Edgeworth's approach to economics and the unifying threads which run through his work. Chapter 2 examines his early work on optimal distribution, culminating in his book on *New and Old Methods of Ethics* (1877). The details of his movement to economics are then discussed in chapter 3, which shows how he became interested in the theory of exchange, which is of course fundamentally associated with distribution. Edgeworth's first and most important contribution to economics was his remarkable monograph entitled *Mathematical Psychics* (1881). Because of the importance of this book, it dominates the discussion of chapters 3 to 5. Chapters 3 and 4 concentrate on his analysis of barter, the importance of indeterminacy, and the effects of introducing additional traders into the market. Chapter 5 shows how this analysis of exchange led Edgeworth to a new approach to, or 'justification' of, utilitarianism, thereby placing his earlier work on optimal distribution in a different light. Despite the fact that *Mathematical Psychics* was highly praised by Jevons and Marshall, many years were to pass before this difficult book was widely appreciated. It is almost certainly cited more often than it is read, but still rewards serious attention.

Chapter 6 then examines Edgeworth's later work on demand theory, the analysis of monopoly, and the theory of distribution. During the 1890s Edgeworth contributed two three-part 'surveys', on the pure theory of taxation and the theory of international values, to the *Economic Journal*. These are examined in chapter 7. A brief review of later developments is then provided in chapter 8. Finally an appendix is included in order to provide some help with the vast number of allusions made in *Mathematical Psychics*, which may not be obvious to the modern reader.

[illegible]

1

Edgeworth's Life and Work

1.1 Biographia

The Family Background

Francis Ysidro Edgeworth was born on 8 February 1845 in Edgeworthstown in County Longford, Ireland. The name had been taken from Edgeworth (now Edgeware) in England, where the family settled in the reign of Elizabeth I.

This once very large Anglo-Irish family provides a rich source for the fascinating account given by Butler and Butler (1927), but the male line has now become almost extinct.

The background into which F. Y. Edgeworth was born was dominated by the 'larger than life' figure of his grandfather Richard Lovell Edgeworth (1744–1817), whose life was very well documented in a two-volume memoir (1820) by his oldest daughter, the famous novelist Maria Edgeworth (1767–1849). Although Richard Lovell moved his family to Edgeworthstown when he inherited the estate, he maintained the contacts he had developed in England with an enormous range of important eighteenth century figures. The extent of family contacts was then further widened by Maria, as shown in the biography by Butler (1972) and in the letters edited by Colvin (1972, 1979). Richard Lovell's many scientific and mechanical experiments were helped by his strong association with the Lunar Society of Birmingham, whose members included Watt, Boulton, Wedgwood, Priestley, Darwin, and Galton. Maria's scientific acquaintances also included Davy, Humboldt, Herschel, Babbage, Hooker and Faraday.

Even the briefest mention of Richard Lovell Edgeworth would be incomplete without reference to his four wives and 22 children (four of whom died in infancy). Each marriage took place only months after the death of the previous wife, and his third wife, Elizabeth Sneyd, was the younger sister of his second wife Honora. The family relationships are complicated by the fact that his fourth wife, Frances Anne Beaufort (1769–1865), was the sister of his friend Sir Francis Beaufort (1774–1857), whose second wife was Honora Edgeworth (1791–1857), a daughter of Richard Lovell Edgeworth by his third wife. Richard Lovell Edgeworth was thus father-in-law and brother-in-law to Francis Beaufort. The marriage of F. Y. Edgeworth's cousin Harriet Jessie Edgeworth (daughter of Richard Lovell's seventh and youngest son Michael Pakenham, 1812–81) to the Rev. Arthur Gray Butler provided links with another large and eminent academic family. These connections extend even further since A. G. Butler's sister, Louisa Butler, married Francis Galton, a cousin of Charles Darwin. Just as Galton's family background was an important influence on his researches into hereditary genius, it is not necessary to look far for the basis of F. Y. Edgeworth's scientific and literary interests, in addition to his strong utilitarianism. These influences will be discussed in more detail in later chapters of this book, especially in chapter 2.

Richard Lovell's sixth son, and seventeenth surviving child, was Francis Beaufort Edgeworth (1809–46), who met his wife, then aged sixteen, in a romantic episode while on the way to Germany to study philosophy, and married within three weeks in 1831. This was Rosa Florentina Eroles, the daughter of a Spanish refugee from Catalonia. It seems that sudden marriages and complex family relationships were almost an Edgeworth tradition. Richard Lovell's great grandfather, returning to Ireland after the death of his wife, stopped a day (Christmas Day) in Chester, and met in the Cathedral a widow who soon became his wife. The children of this couple (from their earlier marriages) later eloped, and their child (R. L. Edgeworth's grandfather) was born while both were still 15 years old.

F. Y. Edgeworth was the fifth son of the marriage between Francis Beaufort Edgeworth and Rosa Florentina Eroles. Francis Beaufort Edgeworth died in 1846, only one year after F. Y. Edgeworth was born. Edgeworth's mixed ancestry, and his strange character, later gave rise to Alfred Marshall's reported dictum that, 'Francis is a charming fellow, but you must be careful with Ysidro' (see Keynes, 1972, p. 265). With his family background and his knowledge of French, German, Spanish and Italian, Edgeworth certainly had wide international sympathies.

Early Life and Career

In contrast with the wealth of information about F. Y. Edgeworth's ancestors, very little is known about his early life. He was educated by tutors in Edgeworthstown until the age of 17, when in 1862 he entered Trinity College Dublin to study languages. In 1867 Edgeworth entered Exeter College, Oxford, but after one term transferred to Magdalen Hall. He later transferred to Balliol in 1868, where he remained for the next two terms, was absent for the next five terms (there were then four per year), but returned in Michaelmas 1869 to take a first in *Literae Humaniares*. During the viva Edgeworth apparently replied, 'shall I answer briefly or at length?', whereupon he spoke for half an hour to convert what was to be a second into a first. However, he did not actually receive his degree until 1873, obtaining his MA in 1877.

There is very little information about his activities in the early 1870s. He was called to the bar in 1877, the same year in which his first book, *New and Old Methods of Ethics*, was published. But it is not clear that he intended to follow a legal career. In her literary biography of Maria Edgeworth, Butler (1972, p. 17, n. 1) points to the emphasis given in several of Maria's books to a legal education, and comments, 'training future landowners in the law was of course a common practice in the 17th and 18th centuries, but not everyone made such a moral virtue of it as the Edgeworths'.

It is known that Edgeworth applied unsuccessfully for a Professorship of Greek at Bedford College, London, in 1875, but later lectured there on English language and literature for a brief period from late 1877 to mid 1878. He had earlier lectured on logic, mental and moral sciences and metaphysics to prospective civil servants of India, at a private institution run by a Mr Walter Wren. In 1880 he applied for a chair of philosophy, also unsuccessfully, but began lecturing on logic to evening classes at King's College London. Soon after the publication of his second book, *Mathematical Psychics*, in 1881, he applied for a professorship of logic, mental and moral philosophy and political economy at Liverpool. Testimonials for two of Edgeworth's applications were given by Jevons (see Black, 1977c, pp. 98, 145) and Marshall. However, Edgeworth had to wait until 1890 until he obtained a professorial appointment. This came after his third and final book *Metretike: or the Method of Measuring Probability and Utility* (1887), and his series of statistical papers beginning in 1883.

Edgeworth had in fact received more recognition for his statistical work, especially in his role as secretary to the British Association Report on Index Numbers, than for his writings on economics. The three volumes (1887, 1888, 1889) on index numbers have been referred to by Pigou (1925a, p. 179) as being, 'of a kind to which the term "classical" may properly be applied'. He was President of section F of the British Association in 1889, a position he held again in 1922. Edgeworth's work on mathematical statistics developed at a considerable rate during the 1880s, and was to take an increasingly important role. Indeed, of about 170 papers which he published, approximately three-quarters were concerned with statistical theory. He became a Guy Medalist (Gold) of the Royal Statistical Society in 1907 and was President of the Society during 1912–14. His main contributions to statistics concern work on inference and the 'law of error', the correlation coefficient, transformations (what he called 'methods of translation'), and the 'Edgeworth expansion'. These contributions cannot be examined here, but it should always be borne in mind that they occupied a great deal of his time and energy. Soon after Edgeworth's death, an assessment of his contribution to mathematical statistics was made by Bowley (1928), and a more recent discussion is contained in Stigler (1978).

Edgeworth's first professorial appointment was at King's College London, where he succeeded Thorold Rogers in the Tooke Chair of Economic Science and Statistics. In the next year, 1891, he again succeeded Rogers, this time to become Drummond Professor and Fellow of All Souls' College, Oxford, a position he held until his retirement in 1922. On his appointment to the Drummond Chair, Edgeworth received a letter from Marshall which began 'Hurrah! Hurrah!! Hurrah!!!' It is interesting to note that Edgeworth gave up his post at King's College, and was succeeded there by the economic historian Cunningham, although Thorold Rogers had held both chairs simultaneously over a long period, having been Tooke Professor 1859–90 and Drummond Professor from 1862 to 1868, and again from 1888 to 1890.

Edgeworth therefore finally settled in Oxford at the age of 46 in one of the most illustrious British chairs in economics. At the same time he became the first editor of the *Economic Journal*. (His role in this position is discussed further below.) After a tremendously creative period of the late 1870s and 1880s, Edgeworth had become firmly established as the leading economist – after Marshall of course – in Britain. But, unlike Marshall at Cambridge, Edgeworth devoted very little energy to improving the undergraduate teaching of economics at Oxford, and seems to have been a very unsuccessful teacher. His influence in Oxford was described briefly by Bowley (1934, p. 123), and at greater length by Price (1946, p. 37) who complained that, 'economics at Oxford looked like slumbering quietly or in effect at least must languish comparatively as it rested, so to say, inert in Edgeworth's keeping. There was no active stir of a resonant hive of busy students gathering honey under his helping regime'. One later exception, which perhaps proves the rule, was of Harrod, who said of his tutorials with Edgeworth, 'we used to sit side by side at a little table, and he'd go through my various diagrams' (see Phelps Brown, 1980, p. 8).

It is indeed impossible to imagine, on the basis of his literary style, how Edgeworth could lecture clearly to a group of undergraduates; and this could not have been helped by his attitude to the subject. As Price (1946, p. 35) again argued, 'Edgeworth . . . convinced that Economics as he conceived it was so intrinsically hard a study that it could not possibly be made popularly plain . . ., increased repellent difficulty'. One cannot help wondering how modern students would react to Edgeworth's precise statement of the simple distinction between a shift and a movement along a demand curve.

> The two meanings of increased demand . . . are most easily and with least liability to logomarchy distinguished as the variation of an ordinate (1) due to displacement of the curve, the abscissa not varying, or (2) corresponding to an increment of the abscissa, the curve being undisturbed. (1925, ii, p. 275, n. 2)

Edgeworth's Character

It does not seem possible to obtain an adequate description of Edgeworth's personality, since there is so little evidence. He certainly inherited 'the Edgeworthstown convention of rather formal good manners and conversation' (Butler, 1972, p. 136). The poet Robert Graves reported that Edgeworth

> avoided conversational English, persistently using words and phrases that one expects to meet only in books. One evening, [T. E.] Lawrence returned from a visit to London, and Edgeworth met him at the gate. 'Was it very caliginous in the Metropolis?'

'Somewhat caliginous, but not altogether inspissated', Lawrence replied gravely. (Graves, R., 1960, p. 247)

The comments of some of Edgeworth's family do, however, provide a little insight into the younger Edgeworth. His aunt, Mrs M. P. Edgeworth, wrote to her sister-in-law (another aunt) Mrs R. Butler (née Harriet Edgeworth) that:

> He is to be one of the 'thinkers' for the rest of the world . . . unless the thoughts are made accessible I am at a loss to see their extreme usefulness . . . Francis said to me he did *think* of teaching as a profession but he is too old to commence a work requiring such flexibility and adaptability of mind to others – qualities wholly absent or underdeveloped as yet in him. (November 1871)

In the same letter there is some hint of Edgeworth being 'delicate', and several years later the same person wrote that, 'Francis Edgeworth looked very well the other evening and it is quite remarkable to see how he improves as he takes to practical work' (November 1874). Unfortunately no other details of his health at this period are available, though it is known that in later years he enjoyed regular exercise including strenuous walking, swimming and cycling.

After Edgeworth's death in 1926, his cousin Mrs A. G. Butler (née Harriet Jessie Edgeworth, daughter of the Mrs M. P. Edgeworth mentioned above) wrote to her daughter that:

> He had become very cousinly and affectionate of late, tho' one could never get very near! Violet and I went last night to the Chapel at Acland home – where he lay on a bier with a sort of stateliness and *keenness* of air, only so *still*. It was a very fine face in its entire repose. Certainly he was one of the cleverest men I have known and the very quickest in mind, I think. (1926)

Mrs Butler also wrote to her son (Professor H. E. Butler) that:

> Mia [Sanderson, Edgeworth's sister] sent a photo of Francis dated I should fancy at least 30 years ago – anyway it represents to me the cousin I knew but slightly, and did *not* like! in the 70s and 80s. He changed and *steadied* and mellowed greatly

> as years went on: tho' I must say 'a charming old gentleman' does not appear to me to describe him. (1926)

Those who knew Edgeworth as a professional colleague have left very little in the way of assessments of his character. Alfred Percival Graves, a contemporary at Trinity College and father of Robert Graves, refers to the antics of some of Edgeworth's brothers and describes briefly an incident in which Edgeworth was 'badly mauled in one of the charges [of a mob outside Trinity] against us' (1931, p. 129). Robert Graves in turn mentioned Edgeworth's 'morbid horror of being touched' (1960, p. 247). A. P. Graves was a founder member of the Savile Club, and although Edgeworth was also a member, there are no records of his date of membership (although it is known that he seconded the nomination of his brother Antonio in 1872). Another friend, the psychologist James Sully (discussed further in later chapters of this book), mentioned in his autobiography his meeting with Edgeworth as a fellow member of the Savile after 1875 (Sully, 1918, p. 164). It is odd that Sully only mentioned Edgeworth by name in one place, but it seems clear that he was obliquely referring to Edgeworth in a number of other contexts (1918, pp. 167, 177–9, 181). There are several references to Edgeworth in the diaries of Beatrice Webb (MacKenzie and MacKenzie, 1983, pp. 283–4); but it is not clear how seriously one should take her suggestion that Edgeworth was an 'admirer' and the comments probably reveal more about Webb than about Edgeworth.

Economists such as Price (1946), Keynes (1972) and Bowley (1934, p. 122) all stressed Edgeworth's generous hospitality, resulting in him having 'the widest personal acquaintance in the world with economists of all nations' (Keynes, 1972, p. 264). However, Keynes suggested that 'His difficult nature . . . cut him off from a full intimacy in any direction. He did not have as much happiness as he might have had' (1972, p. 237). The difficulty in obtaining a clearer view of his character is reflected in the following summary by Keynes.

> On anyone who knew Edgeworth he must have made a strong individual impression as a person. But it is scarcely possible to portray him to those who did not. He was kind, affectionate, modest, self-deprecatory, humorous, with a sharp and candid eye for human nature; he was also reserved, angular, complicated, proud, and touchy, elaborately polite, courteous

to the point of artificiality, absolutely unbending and unyielding in himself to the pressure of the outside world. (1972, p. 265)

Having briefly described the main details of Edgeworth's life and career it is useful at this stage to consider the way in which he approached the subject of economics, his attitude to the results of pure theory, and his style of writing. Edgeworth's books and papers were all characterized by his highly individual and difficult style; sometimes amusing, occasionally acerbic, always scholarly, usually terse, often eloquent, always highly allusive, and of course frequently mathematical. It has been all too easy for later commentators to misrepresent his views and basic approach, without any deliberate intention to do so. The following section therefore introduces the main features of his work, and it will sometimes be necessary to return to these aspects in later chapters.

1.2 Edgeworth's Approach to Economics

The Role of Mathematics

To the casual reader, probably the single most dominant characteristic of Edgeworth's approach to economics is that it is mathematical. Although Walras and Jevons had both used elementary mathematics as an important part of their work, Edgeworth's writings were characterized by a considerably deeper knowledge, and a much more original use, of techniques. Edgeworth's particular innovations, and his mathematical training, are discussed later in this book, but it is necessary to discuss at this stage some general features of his use of mathematics.

His preoccupation with mathematics was notorious. It has been well illustrated by Bowley (1934, p. 119), who told the following anecdote to show how difficult it was to 'turn the conversation' from mathematical and statistical subjects. As a party of economists, including Edgeworth, was cycling out of Cambridge in 1904, Cannan drew alongside Bowley and said, 'Put on the pace, Bowley, he can't talk mathematics at more than 12 miles an hour'. However, most readers would surely agree that Edgeworth's mathematics moved at considerable speed, and he rarely slowed down to give directions to those in danger of losing their way. It is difficult to know just why Edgeworth gave so little guidance, particularly as he so often felt the need to provide an 'apology' for the use of mathematics. But it is interesting that on two occasions (1877, p. 60; 1881, p. 139) he quoted some of the following lines, without acknowledging the source, from the poet Alexander Pope:

> Trace science then, with modesty thy guide;
> First strip off all her equipage of pride.
> Deduct what is but vanity or dress,
> Or learning's luxury, or idleness:
> Mere tricks to show the stretch of human brain.
> (Pope, *Essay on Man*, 2nd Epistle)

It may be thought that Edgeworth eventually turned to economics simply because he saw in it a good source of applications of his mathematical training. However, as shown in more detail in chapters 2 and 3 of this book, he came to economics from moral philosophy; the central question of distributive justice (rather than simply the application of mathematics) dominated his whole attitude towards economic subjects. His main argument was that mathematics provided powerful assistance to 'unaided' reason, and could check the conclusions reached by other methods. Thus:

> He that will not verify his conclusions as far as possible by mathematics, as it were bringing the ingots of common sense to be assayed and coined at the mint of the sovereign science, will hardly realise the full value of what he holds, will want a measure of what it will be worth in however slightly altered circumstances, a means of conveying and making it current. (1881, p. 3)

Edgeworth thus considered it his duty to point to any fallacies, and in an 'age of luxuriant speculation, when novel theories teem in so many new economic journals' (1925, ii, p. 282), there was much work to do. The regular flow of criticism, aided by Edgeworth's easy access to publication, has led later commentators to suggest that he was only interested in producing *curiosa* and 'illuminating the obscure with the more obscure' (Keynes, 1972, p. 264). But there was, as this book will demonstrate, a considerable unity in the bulk of his work; this has tended however to become lost from sight due to the unyielding abstract nature of his writing.

There is of course no doubt that Edgeworth attached high priority to the use of mathematics, contrasting sharply with Marshall, who later wrote to Bowley that 'Edgeworth might have done something great at it [economics]: but he has crushed his instincts between the cog wheels of his mathematical machinery' (March, 1901). These comments were obviously designed to influence Bowley, and had little success, but the contrast between Edgeworth and Marshall was neatly summarized by Pigou as follows:

> During some thirty years until their recent deaths in honoured age, the two outstanding names in English economics were Marshall . . . and Edgeworth . . . Edgeworth, the tool-maker, gloried in his tools . . . Marshall, on the other hand, had what almost amounted to an obsession for hiding his tools away. (Pigou and Robertson, 1931, p. 3)

This contrast between Edgeworth and Marshall is just one aspect of a more general difference between their approaches. Although both men turned to economics from mathematics and moral philosophy, their backgrounds in these latter subjects were, however, also very different. Marshall had a greater element of 'feeling' or 'warmth', to use Viner's terms (1958, p. 252). He generally used biological analogies, and was concerned with developing *maxims*. In contrast Edgeworth's interest was intellectual; he generally used mechanical analogies, and was more concerned with developing *theorems*. In order to justify the use of very complex mathematics to generate what often seemed very narrow results, Edgeworth argued that the 'road, though short, is so slippery as to require every precaution' and stated:

> The case is like that of the 'swell' in *Punch*, who, about to enter a hansom, inquires solicitously of the driver whether he has got a good horse. 'Yes, Sir; very good 'oss'. 'Aw – then dwive to next door'. (1925, ii, p. 286)

Edgeworth and Methodology

Several aspects of Edgeworth's methodological position can be discussed briefly at this point. His approach was of course strongly deductive and a priori, and it must be remembered that in the 1880s and 1890s such a position was facing a great deal of criticism, especially from the 'historical school' of economists. Edgeworth therefore felt obliged to provide many defences of the deductive method, and these often took the form of showing how other economists had advocated its use (his appeal to authority will be discussed later). Edgeworth's remark in his inaugural lecture at Oxford in 1891, that 'like the cultivated Athenian, we should eschew the invidious disparagement of each others' pursuits' (1925, i, p. 11) would seem to be an allusion to the controversy between the historical and deductive schools.

His interest in the natural sciences often led him to make comparisons with scientific 'laws', and especially to show that the physical sciences also relied on abstraction and approximation. For example, after discussing the fact that an engineer making a tunnel may assume that gravel is a 'continuous substance', but that in considering the progress of a worm through the same substance, the same assumption cannot be made, he commented 'it cannot be considered as paradoxical that a less exact science should rest in part on similarly inexact axioms' (1925, ii, p. 390).

Edgeworth carefully argued that the assumptions used in economics are often untestable, and he therefore took precautions against the accusation of 'plucking assumptions from the air'. He was conscious of the fact that the difficulty is in making the *crucial* abstractions which make the particular problem under consideration tractable, but which are not question begging. His attitude to many a priori assumptions was directly related to his approach to statistical inference. In *Mathematical Psychics*, for example, he referred to 'the first principle of probabilities, according to which cases about which we are equally undecided . . . count as equal' (1881, p. 99). This was then transferred to economics. The appropriate assumption was that all feasible values (say of elasticities) were equally likely, until evidence is obtained. The importance of equal a priori probabilities to Edgeworth's approach will again be emphasized in chapter 5, when examining his special 'justification' of utilitarianism as a principle of distributive justice.

The presumption in favour of equal a priori probabilities was, however, 'liable to be superseded by specific evidence . . . There is required, I think, . . . in order to override the a priori probability, either very definite specific evidence, or the concensus of high authorities' (1925, ii, p. 391). This quotation also helps to illustrate Edgeworth's attitude to authority and his many allusions to the views of other leading economists, though he was hardly 'tongue-tied by authority'. One method of showing that an assumption was sensible for the problem at hand was to show that other authorities had made similar assumptions. Price (1946, p. 38) refers to the comparatively few books, on his 'scanty shelves', which were 'copiously interleaved . . . . with slips of paper, inserted, characteristically, I suppose, to facilitate prompt reference to authority for . . . support of tentative opinion waveringly advanced'. Edgeworth's attitude to authority can in fact also be related to his utilitarianism, and this neglected feature will be discussed briefly in the following chapter.

Theory and Policy

Edgeworth regularly stressed the importance of the 'interposing chasms' between theoretical results and their application to policy problems. Specific examples will be given in later chapters of this book, but here it is worth pointing out that his outlook was much more than one of caution; his approach is more accurately described as being *negative*. This is partly reflected in the fact that in *Mathematical Psychics* (1881, pp. 95, 129) he twice quotes, as always without acknowledging the source, Pope's line, 'Reason is here no guide, but still a guard' (from *Essay on Man*, 2nd Epistle, Argument III). The negative attitude is also linked to his view, discussed above, of the role of mathematics in exposing fallacies, and was explicitly stated in his inaugural lecture in Oxford, 1891, as follows:

> in the race of the sciences we are as it were handicapped by having to start at a considerable distance behind the position of mere nescience. An effort is required to remove prejudices worse than ignorance; a great part of the career of our science has consisted in surmounting preliminary fallacies. (1925, i, p. 5)

In view of the fact that Edgeworth has sometimes been accused of building on 'shifting sands', because of the problems associated with the measurement of utility, the following statement is worth reproducing as an indication of his stress on negative results. This occurs in the course of his analysis of taxation, where the criterion of minimum sacrifice (discussed in more detail in chapter 7) does not alone provide a simple tax formula. He stated:

> Yet the premises, however inadequate to the deduction of a definite formula, may suffice for a certain negative conclusion. The ground which will not serve as the foundation of the elaborate edifice designed may yet be solid enough to support a battering-ram capable of being directed against simpler edifices in the neighbourhood. (1925, ii, p. 261)

It seems that this feature of Edgeworth's work was a reflection of an attitude which extended to many other aspects of his life; indeed Price (1946, p. 33) mentioned that he could hardly ever obtain from his 'balancing friend' a definite conclusion on any matter, 'except occasionally the damnation of an outrageous fallacy'.

Editorship of the Economic Journal

The founding of the British Economic Association (which in 1902 became the Royal Economic Society) and the publication of Marshall's *Principles of Economics* in 1890 make that year an important one in British economics. The main contribution of the Association was its publication of a specialist *Economic Journal*, of which Edgeworth was the first editor. In fact he was editor or co-editor from its first issue until his death in 1926. He was supported by Henry Higgs from 1892 to 1905 (when the latter became the Prime Minister's Private Secretary), with further assistance provided at a later stage by Alfred Hoare. Keynes was a co-editor for 15 years and, after the deaths of Edgeworth and Hoare, wrote that 'an old and beloved civilisation has departed, and we hear the barbarians at the gate' (1972, p. 313). Contrary to what might be expected from Edgeworth's reputation as an unworldly figure, Keynes (1972, p. 264) reported that he was 'business like, and dependable in the conduct of all routine matters', and his work as editor was highly praised by Marshall (see Coats, 1968, p. 365). There were of course awkward episodes, as for example when Edgeworth was charged with discourtesy by John Rae (he was acquitted by the Council of the Association), and when he refused to publish a rejoinder by Cunningham to a reply by Marshall to Cunningham's attack upon him (see Coats, 1968, p. 367; 1967, p. 712, n. 10). But on the whole his reign as editor was a calm one.

There is no doubt that Edgeworth's position as editor of the *Economic Journal* had a significant effect on his future economic writings. It enabled him to combine both his critical attitude and his appetite for a very wide range of reading. He contributed no less than 32 book reviews, and in sending books to other reviewers he would include 'apposite remarks on particular points in the text' (Bowley, 1934, p. 123). These reviews should also be placed beside his 17 reviews in the *Academy*, and 131 articles in Palgrave's *Dictionary of Economics*. Some of his *Economic Journal* reviews were collected in the third volume of his *Papers Relating to Political Economy* (1925), and make interesting and sometimes entertaining reading. Furthermore, Edgeworth's later articles in the *Economic Journal* (such as those on international trade and taxation) took the form of extended commentaries on all the contemporary work of any value. However, his own original suggestions are, as a result, often rather obscurely buried in footnotes. This was unfortunate. More harm may have arisen from the dissipation of his energy on reviews; compare his output with that of Marshall, who wrote only two book reviews. Furthermore, the easy access to publication meant that he was not really forced to 'polish' his work, thus intensifying his problem of communication. Edgeworth did not unfortunately have the advantage enjoyed by his aunt Maria, of help with the polishing and revision of manuscripts from other members of her family (see Butler, 1972, pp. 147, 291). His three monographs had all been published at his own expense, so that Edgeworth never seemed to have been in the frustrating but valuable position of having to respond to editors' and referees' comments. As a result, he never reached a wide audience, the unity in his work was concealed, and most modern readers are left with the impression that he was only interested in isolated technical problems of analysis.

This impression is not completely removed by a perusal of Edgeworth's three volumes of collected *Papers* which he selected and edited, and which were published by the Royal Economic Society when he was 80 years old. A number of deletions were made from some of the original papers, 'on the ground of what may be called excessive elaboration. It is not intended thereby to attribute excess to the original publication. What is worth saying once may not be worth repeating' (1925, i, p. vii). But the selection only very partially serves as the treatise which, by temperament, he would never produce, although it is an invaluable collection. The success of this well-reviewed publication seems to have given Edgeworth, 'as much pleasure as surprise' (Keynes, 1972, p. 263).

When discussing, in *Mathematical Psychics*, the results of barter among a large number of competitors in a market, Edgeworth again borrowed a line from Alexander Pope's *Essay on Man* (Epistle 1). His description of the market as, 'A mighty maze! but not without a plan' could just as appropriately be applied to Edgeworth's many contributions to economics. It is the purpose of the following chapters to attempt to provide a description of the general 'plan' of Edgeworth's work, and to provide some guidance along the slippery paths.

Further Reading

The best sources for the early history of the Edgeworth family are Maria Edgeworth's memoir of her father (1820) and the collection by Butler and Butler (1927). Colvin (1972, 1979) gives many useful biographical details about members of the large family, and Mrs Colvin kindly provided the extracts from the letters of H. J. Butler, quoted above. The literary biography of Maria, by Butler (1972), is strongly recommended, and this helps to correct the earlier reaction against the influence of Richard Lovell Edgeworth, exemplified in the popular accounts of Lawless (1904) and Clarke (1949). For a brief genealogical table linking Charles Darwin, Francis Galton, and Edgeworth, see Farebrother (1983); see also Halsey (1976, p. 44), and Annan (1955, pp. 264–71). R. L. Edgeworth's scientific activities and connections are documented in the valuable account of the 'Lunar Society' by Schofield (1963). On F. Y. Edgeworth there is very little, other than the references in the text and further details at the end of chapter 2. Bowley's paper (1934), and Keynes's essay (1972) were for long the major sources. The discussions of Edgeworth at various points in Price's memoirs (1946) are of interest; see also Price (1926) and Bonar (1926). His collected papers were reviewed by Pigou (1925a) and Fisher (1925). Kendall (1970) concentrates on Edgeworth's contribution to statistics, and it should be noted that his account of Francis Beaufort Edgeworth's planned trip to Germany with his nephew T. L. Beddoes, and meeting with his future wife, is incorrect (but see Butler and Butler, 1927, p. 248). For a brief review of Edgeworth's life and work see also Creedy (1981). On Edgeworth's statistics, the paper by Pratt (1976) is also of interest. Edgeworth's international sympathies were stressed by Keynes, who wrote, 'I am sure that there was no economist in England better read than he in foreign literature. He added to this what must have been the widest personal acquaintance in the world with economists of all nations' (1972, p. 264; see also Bowley, 1934, p. 122). The letters to Edgeworth from Marshall are held in the Special Collections section of the London School of Economics Library, which also has Edgeworth's own copy of *Mathematical Psychics*. This however contains only a few marginal comments and corrections, as indicated in the appendix. Edgeworth's attitude to 'authority' (and the link with his utilitarian philosophy) has sometimes been misinterpreted; for example, Keynes said that 'his ostensible reverence for authority . . . led him to waste an abundance of time' (1972, p. 265). In fact most of Edgeworth's footnote references to authorities seem to have been drawn directly from memory, as they are often incomplete and sometimes inaccurate; on his memory see Keynes (1972, p. 284), Bowley (1934, p. 123) and Price (1926, p. 28). The general standards with regard to citations were fairly low at that time, but this does raise special problems for readers of Edgeworth. Further details regarding *Mathematical Psychics* have therefore been provided in the appendix to this book.

The character of the *Economic Journal* during Edgeworth's period as editor may be seen from the review by Jha (1973), who stresses the importance of applied work. Edgeworth's refusal to publish a review by Barone of Wicksteed (1894) will be mentioned in chapter 6. It has been suggested that Edgeworth's own review of Hobson and Mummery's *Physiology of Industry* (1888) led to the dismissal of Hobson as a London University Extension Lecturer (see Hobson, 1938, p. 30; Hutchison, 1953, p. 118). Yet, as Burrows (1978, pp. 12–13) showed, Hobson continued to give many courses in economics as an Extension Lecturer. In the diary of Beatrice Webb there are only three brief references to Edgeworth (covering June 1889), and these are open to several interpretations. In the first entry she referred to Edgeworth as 'a gentle-natured and intellectual man with queer cramped nature, excessively polite and diffident in manner, formal and exact in phraseology – an old admirer and a present lover!' (see MacKenzie and MacKenzie, 1983, p. 283). Keynes reported that when he asked Edgeworth why he had never written a treatise, he 'answered, with his characteristic smile and chuckle, that large scale enterprises, such as treatises and marriage, had never appealed to him' (1972, p. 262). Keynes also wrote that although Edgeworth never married, 'it was not for want of susceptibility. His difficult nature, not his conception of life, cut him off from a full intimacy in any direction' (1972, p. 266). Robert Graves also reported that he and Edgeworth

> planned to collaborate in a burlesque on contemporary writers, in the style of a Government Blue Book . . . when he asked at the Stationery Office for a Blue-book, the clerk asked, 'Which Blue-book, we have hundreds.'
> 'Whichever you like.'
> Mistaking his indifference for guilty embarrassment, the clerk handed him the report of a Royal Commission on Venereal Disease. (1960, p. 247)

2

Early Work: Methods of Ethics

It has been seen that very little is known about Edgeworth's activities between graduation and being called to the Bar in 1877. The same year also saw the publication of his first privately printed book on *New and Old Methods of Ethics*, which was for long thought to be his first publication. However, a search directed by H. G. Johnson, and mentioned by Kendall (1970), revealed a critical note written by Edgeworth in *Mind* in 1876, in which he discussed Matthew Arnold's views of Butler (a typographical error gives the author's initials as T. Y. instead of F. Y.). Although this early note is less than one page in length, it does, as shown below, throw some light on Edgeworth's early views. This chapter concentrates on Edgeworth's early work before he turned to economics, an appreciation of which is crucial for a proper understanding of his later contributions. The main focus of this early work was to examine in some detail the implications of utilitarianism for the 'optimal' distribution of resources, and Edgeworth's special and original contribution was to apply advanced mathematics to this problem. It is clear that, despite the absence of outward signs of activity, Edgeworth's studies covered, in some considerable depth, a very wide range of literature. Once he managed to 'find' a subject which suited his special combination of skills, progress was very rapid indeed.

The examination of Edgeworth's early work is important for several reasons. It has long been fashionable to describe Edgeworth, along with other late nineteenth century economists, in very simple terms as a 'cardinalist' who supported the simplistic demonstration that utilitarianism implies perfect equality. For example, Samuelson considerably oversimplified the position when he wrote, 'to a man like Edgeworth, steeped as he was in the utilitarian tradition, individual utility – nay social utility – was as real as his morning jam'

(1947, p. 206). But this neglects the many different strands in his work, in particular the influence of contemporary psychological research and the impact of evolutionary ideas. Both aspects led to explicit consideration of differences between individuals, and changes which take place over time.

Section 2.1 first considers the background to, and development of, Edgeworth's early utilitarianism, where it is seen that at this stage his approach is eclectic rather than original. He is seen to draw on the same influences which were very important to other late Victorian scholars. A consideration of this background also sheds some light on his attitude towards 'authority' (briefly discussed in the previous chapter). As already indicated, Edgeworth's special contribution was to clarify, using advanced mathematics, the implications of the objective of utility maximization for the distribution of income and 'happiness'. This work is discussed in section 2.2. An important feature of Edgeworth's analysis was his introduction, into one area of literature (moral philosophy), of techniques that were developed in an entirely different area (mathematics). These early technical contributions are examined in section 2.3. This 'importation' of methods is of course relevant to discussions of the development or 'advance' of particular subjects or 'disciplines', and in this respect it is important to recognize that Edgeworth used techniques of analysis which he had *already* acquired for other purposes, or under different incentives. In Edgeworth's case a further interest arises from the fact that he seems to have had no systematic training or formal education in mathematics. An attempt to investigate his mathematical training is thus reported in section 2.4.

2.1 Edgeworth's Early Utilitarianism

The Family Influence

In searching for the origins of the 'Benthamite' strand in Edgeworth's utilitarianism there is no need to look further than his remarkable family background. The most important members from this point of view are his grandfather Richard Lovell Edgeworth (1774–1817), and his aunt Maria Edgeworth (1767–1849), described by F. Y. Edgeworth as 'a very plain old lady with a delightful face'. Richard Lovell's wide range of contacts included Bentham and his leading continental followers, and Bentham's translator Dumont gave advice to Maria when she was completing her *Memoir* of her father. Another friend was Joseph Priestley (1733–1804), in whose *Essay on Government* (1786), found in a circulating library attached to a coffee-house in Oxford, Bentham found the phrase, 'the greatest happiness of the greatest number'.

Utilitarianism pervades Maria's novels, and a clear statement of Richard Lovell and Maria Edgeworth's utilitarianism is also found, for example, in one of their tales from *The Parent's Assistant*, where two children are advised by their father about the most important virtues. They are told, 'the most useful, I think, should come first, and you might, I believe, arrange them all by their degrees of usefulness or utility'. On the question of what determines usefulness, the answer is that, 'we must know what contributes most to the happiness of the greatest number of people, and for the greatest length of time'. Maria later wrote of her father that:

> He not only estimated what every object of fancy and taste would cost, but he accustomed himself to consider what the actual enjoyment of the indulgence would be. Carefully analysing his own feelings, he observed how much . . . our real tastes are gratified by the purchase or pursuit of many things (1820, ii, p. 422).

The 'Sovereign Principle'

Edgeworth was also naturally influenced by the major, and very strong, debates in the last half of the nineteenth century between the familiar 'isms' of egoism, evolutionism, idealism, intuitionism, and of course utilitarianism. Edgeworth's brand of utilitarianism became extremely eclectic, and embraced the majority of the above principles (except for those of the Hegelian idealists) while regarding utilitarianism as the 'sovereign principle'. He simply took a very dismissive attitude towards the idealists, referring to the 'false friend and dire foe of hedonism . . . the voluptuary and the hegelian' (1877, p. 70). It will be seen that one of Edgeworth's major influences during this period was the great Cambridge philosopher Henry Sidgwick (1838–1900). Sidgwick's strongest critic, F. H. Bradley, was mentioned only once by Edgeworth in 1877 (p. 9, n. 2), and in 1881 his dismissal of the Hegelians was strong even by Edgeworth's standards: '. . . blind to truth in her clearest manifestations . . . ignorant of his ignorance and vain of his inanity' (1881, p. 97). In view of this antipathy, it is interesting to remember that Edgeworth's father was in fact on his way to Germany to study philosophy when he met his future wife and quickly changed his plans.

The main point of Edgeworth's first publication (the note in *Mind* of 1876), was to argue that egoism and utilitarianism could be subsumed under the same principle. Egoism had been examined at length by Joseph Butler (1692–1752), who had been Bishop of Bristol (1738), Dean of St Pauls (1740) and Dean of Durham (1750). Matthew Arnold had argued that Butler's term 'self love' should be interpreted to mean 'the pursuit of our temporal good'. However, Edgeworth believed Butler to be saying, 'duty and interest are perfectly coincident; for the most part in this world, but entirely and in every instance, if we take in the future and the whole' (1876, p. 571). Thus if individuals take a much longer view of the effects of their actions, extending beyond their lifetime on earth, they will consider the welfare of others. In view of the importance of Sidgwick to Edgeworth, it is also worth noting in this connection the statement of Schneewind (1977, p. 418) that, 'To no major historical figure does Sidgwick have closer affinities than to Bishop Butler. His reconstruction of Butler's insistence that concern for one's own good and concern for the good of others both equally embody the same sort of practical rationality is only the most noticeable of the similarities in their thought.' In view also of the importance of Jevons to Edgeworth (as explained in chapter 3), it may not be inappropriate to mention Gladstone's praise of some of Jevons's work as being 'Butlerian' (see Black, 1977a, p. 38).

In understanding Edgeworth's attitude here, it is useful to mention that he generally made a distinction between what he referred to as 'impure' and 'pure' utilitarianism. In the latter case individuals are assumed to be concerned with the welfare of society as a whole. The former case in fact corresponds more closely with a 'short term' version of egoism. For example, he later considered that economic exchange could usefully be analysed in terms of 'jostling egoists'. But he believed that ultimately individuals would become pure utilitarians. A reason for believing that individuals would make such a 'transition' was later to be developed by Edgeworth in the form of his 'contractarian' justification of utilitarianism as the appropriate principle of distributive justice, but discussion of this is best delayed until chapter 5. In his early work he relied instead mainly on an argument based on the effects of evolution in developing sympathy and appreciation of the 'higher pleasures'.

Edgeworth's views of a broadly defined utilitarianism as the 'sovereign' principle were made somewhat clearer in his first short book called *New and Old Methods of Ethics: or Physical Ethics and Methods of Ethics* (1877). This book was directly stimulated by Sidgwick's *Methods of Ethics* (1874), and the review of the latter by Alfred Barratt (1877). Barratt had earlier published an attempt to apply psychological work to moral philosophy, in his book called *Physical Ethics* (1869); hence the subtitle of Edgeworth's book. The description by Keynes of Edgeworth's first book could just as well be applied to his other two books:

> Edgeworth's peculiarities of style, his brilliance of phrasing, his obscurity of connection, his inconclusiveness of aim, his restlessness of direction, his courtesy, his caution, his shrewdness, his wit, his subtlety, his learning, his reserve – all are there full-grown. Quotations from the Greek tread on the heels of the differential calculus . . . (Keynes, 1972, p. 257)

The first part of *New and Old Methods of Ethics* attempted to synthesize the various approaches to moral philosophy so that they could be subsumed under utilitarianism. The role of evolution in the transition from impure to pure utilitarianism was stated by Edgeworth as follows: 'The egoist, then, may have the power and the motive to cultivate a desire for the general good, not, indeed to the pitch of pure utilitarianism, but to a degree asymptotically approaching it, in the progress of evolution' (1877, p. 33). This link with evolutionism was also strongly stated by Edgeworth when he reviewed Leslie Stephen's book on *The Science of Ethics* (1882), and argued that 'two great streams' of evolutionism and utilitarianism 'become ultimately convergent' (1882, p. 446). An important part of his argument was of course that tastes are not fixed, but can change over time. The influence of the work of Darwin and Galton on this aspect of his early work is very clear, and will be mentioned again in chapter 5.

It is perhaps worth stressing at this point that Edgeworth's attitude to 'pure' utilitarianism does not correspond at all with the 'natural harmony' theories. The view that the pursuit of self-interest would lead, via the interdependencies of a complex exchange economy, to a situation which could be described as socially optimal, was quite different. Indeed, it will be seen later that Edgeworth strongly argued that the more usual situation would be one of conflict, thereby requiring arbitration based on utilitarian principles.

Research in Experimental Psychology

A further important aspect of Edgeworth's early utilitarianism was his wide knowledge of the (mainly continental) work in experimental psychology. In this books of 1877 and 1881 there are many references to the work of Delboeuf, Fechner, Helmholtz, Weber and Wundt, all major figures in experimental psychology (see the appendix for further details). These references occur in the context of discussing the nature of utility functions, and although Edgeworth at this time was not aware of the earlier work of Jevons, the same range of psychological work was also important to Jevons. This work was considered relevant because it had attempted to measure experimentally the responsiveness of subjects to different types of stimuli. It seems surprising that this aspect of their work has been neglected. Thus Jevons's son had to remind Keynes of the importance of psychological research to W. S. Jevons's work (see Keynes, 1972, p. 153). After mentioning the work of Wundt, Weber, Fechner and Helmholtz, even Schumpeter (1954, p. 796, n. 1) makes the surprising statement that, 'it has not so far occurred to economists to explore the opportunities this line of research might conceivably offer'. Furthermore Stigler (1965, p. 114) said that Edgeworth 'made no real use of Fechner's theory', but this statement is true only if narrowly interpreted to mean that he rejected the logarithmic utility function suggested by Fechner.

A significant example of the influence of such work on Edgeworth's approach to the utility function concerns the assumption of additivity. It is usual, as in Stigler (1965, p. 106), Hutchison (1953, p. 306) and Blaug (1968, p. 330), to cite *Mathematical Psychics* (1881) as the place where Edgeworth first introduced the more general form of the utility function. But in 1877 he explicitly suggested, in connection with Fechner, that an additive form would not be appropriate. He stated:

> As we ascend from the region of sensations, we may seem to come first to what Fechner calls relations between sensations. For in the arithmetic of hedonism, the whole is not to be equalled to the sum of the parts but to the sum + the relations of the parts. (1877, p. 72)

When Edgeworth later turned to the economic analysis of exchange, after meeting Jevons some time in 1879, it was therefore only natural that he should use the more general function. The neglect of this aspect of Edgeworth's early work even extends to Viner, who stated, 'the only citation to the Weber–Fechner law that I have encountered in the early literature of the utility theory is by Edgeworth in his *Mathematical Psychics*' (1958, p. 183, n. 21).

Edgeworth's knowledge of the psychological research was undoubtedly helped by his friendship with James Sully. The two met after Sully became a member of the Savile Club in 1875; Edgeworth acknowledged Sully's help with his *New and Old Methods of Ethics*, and was in turn thanked by Sully for reading the proofs of the latter's *Pessimism: A History and a Critique* (1877). When Edgeworth later suggested that 'higher' pleasures are 'most pleasurable' (1879, p. 395; 1881, p. 58), he referred to the 'scientific statement' of this view by Sully. The latter's wide range of contacts was acknowledged by Sidgwick when he wrote that Sully was 'probably the one Englishman known to German professors as a writer on physiological psychology' (see Sidgwick and Sidgwick, 1906, p. 516). Sully will again be discussed in section 2.4 and in chapter 3.

The Role of Authority

A further, often neglected, aspect of Edgeworth's utilitarianism is his attitude towards 'authority'. This attitude (briefly introduced in the previous chapter) has often been misunderstood in the past; for example, Keynes suggested that, 'his ostensible reverence for authority and disinclination to say anything on his own responsibility led him to waste an abundance of time' (1972, p. 265).

An important issue which concerned early utilitarians, for whom happiness was the ultimate end, involved the nature of inductive evidence about the consequences of acts. The problem was that most people cannot know the full consequences of their acts, so that certain rules of moral conduct must be accepted and followed. (This contrasts with intuitionism where individuals are assumed to have 'immediate consciousness' of moral rules). In arriving at such rules, the opinions of special highly regarded individuals are taken by most people to be credible though it may not be possible to show conclusively that they are 'correct'. Edgeworth argued, for example, that 'we ought to defer even to the undemonstrated dicta and opinions of the wise, who have a power of mental vision acquired by experience' (1925, ii, p. 149). In 1877 Edgeworth took exception to Sidgwick's low estimate of the value of authority, and argued that authority 'may afford more than commonplace advice to common man' (1877, p. 27). In fact in questions of moral philosophy Edgeworth always regarded Sidgwick himself as the highest authority (see 1925, ii, pp. 147–52), just as he later came to regard Marshall as the highest authority in Economics. Edgeworth's views on the necessity of authority, which derived from this particular utilitarian concern, can be seen to be in line with those of John Austin and George Cornewall Lewis, both of whom are mentioned by him in *Mathematical Psychics* (1881, pp. 103, 126; see also the appendix to this book).

In his later economic and statistical work he was very conscious of the fact that it was often necessary to make a priori assumptions which were not capable of being tested. Edgeworth therefore appealed to authority as almost equivalent to more conventional types of evidence. He wished to show that his abstractions were sensible for the problem at hand, and one way of doing this was to show that others had made similar assumptions.

Having considered the wide range of influences on Edgeworth's early work it is worth stressing that Marshall's views, though not quite those of Edgeworth, were also very eclectic. Marshall's early interests were of course also very wide, and covered some of the same ground. For example Whitaker (1977, p. 193, n. 84) quotes Wesley Mitchell as saying that Marshall's 'technical analysis smacks of Bentham; his hope for the future of Darwin. Perhaps he thought that Spencer had really reconciled the two conceptions of behaviour.' Herbert Spencer had of course applied evolutionary doctrines to moral philosophy, most notably in his two volume *Principles of Ethics* (1879). Mitchell's statement suggests a close similarity between Edgeworth and Marshall, but in fact Marshall was much more sympathetic to idealism. As Whitaker points out:

> The chief formative influence appears to have been a heady but turgid mixture of German Idealism, Spencerian evolutionism, and utilitarianism, the latter derived from a close reading of Bentham and Mill and from the personal influence of Sidgwick. (1977, p. 194)

It is evident that Whitaker's following comment applies equally to Edgeworth when comparing two generations of economists: 'The broadness of Marshall's concerns illustrates by contrast the narrowness of ours' (1977, p. 197).

2.2 The Optimal Distribution

Edgeworth's attempt in the first part of *New and Old Methods of Ethics* to provide a synthesis of the various approaches in such a way that they are concerned with the same ultimate ends provided the groundwork for his really original contribution. In the second part of the book, Edgeworth applied mathematical techniques to the problem of determining the optimal utilitarian distribution. In view of the considerable respect which Edgeworth had for Sidgwick as an 'authority' it is worth considering the following quotation from Sidgwick, which Edgeworth reproduced (1877, p. 35, n. 1):

> That our practical utilitarian reasonings may be rough is no reason for not making them as accurate as the case admits; and we shall be more likely to succeed in this, if we keep before our minds as distinctly as possible the strict type of calculation that we should have to make, if all the relevant considerations could be estimated with mathematical precision. (Sidgwick, 1874, book IV, ch. 1, §2)

It is indeed this kind of argument which lies behind much of Edgeworth's later mathematical economics, and is, in a slightly different form, still used by modern economists; see, for example, Atkinson and Stiglitz (1980, p. 456), who refer to their exploration of the 'grammar of arguments'.

Maximum Total Utility

After discussing, in mathematical terms, the possible meanings of 'the greatest happiness of the greatest number' (1877, pp. 36–9), Edgeworth considers the nature of the utility function. He explicitly argues, on the authority of Fechner, that the first derivative is positive and the second derivative is negative. It is important to stress the point that Edgeworth's assumptions about the signs of these derivatives were based directly on the results of experimental psychologists. Thus:

> The sort of proof initiated by Fechner is not peculiar to the Fechnerian law, but may be extended to an indefinite number of similar formulae, involving, instead of the logarithm, some function which shares with the logarithm the following

> properties; that the first differential is positive, the second differential negative for all values of the variable, or at least all with which we are concerned. (1877, p. 40)

Edgeworth then writes the utility function, π, as k (the capacity for pleasure) multiplied by $\{f(y) - f(\beta)\}$, where y represents the 'means of pleasure' and β is the threshold or, 'the value of stimulus for which there is sense of pleasure at all' (1877, p. 42). It is of course assumed that $f(y) > f(\beta)$ throughout, although the question of whether the 'least well off' person experiences positive happiness is considered later, and also in (1881, p. 73). The utility of the ith person can thus be written as $k_i\{f(y_i) - f(\beta_i)\}$.

The first problem is to find the distribution of y for which total utility is maximized. Edgeworth set this up as follows: 'Given a certain quantity of stimulus to be distributed among a given set of sentients . . . to find the law of distribution productive of the greatest quantity of pleasure' (1877, p. 43). He then takes the simplest case first, 'where all the elements are equal as touching sensibility and capacity for pleasure'. Thus $k_i = k$ and $\beta_i = \beta$, for all i. When Edgeworth says that the total 'quantity of stimulus' is assumed to be fixed, this of course means that $\Sigma_i y_i$ is fixed, at say Y. In modern terms the mathematical problem is to maximize

$$k\sum_i \{f(y_i) - f(\beta)\}$$

subject to the linear constraint that

$$\sum_i y_i = Y$$

This can be handled, using basic Lagrange multiplier techniques, by introducing the multiplier λ, say, and maximizing

$$k\sum_i \{f(y_i) - f(\beta)\} - \lambda\left(\sum_i y_i - Y\right)$$

Having very quickly set up the problem, Edgeworth does not bother to explain the procedure, but continues:

> The pleasure of the whole may be represented by $k\{f(y_1) - f(\beta)\} + k\{f(y_2) - f(\beta)\} + k\{f(y_3) - f(\beta)\} +$ &c where y_1, y_2, y_3, &c., are variables, depending only on the condition that

> $y_1 + y_2 + y_3 + \&c = \text{given}$. In order, then, that the whole may be a maximum $k\{f(y_1) + f(y_2) + \&c\} - c(y_1 + y_2 + \&c)$ must be a maximum: the solution of which problem (since f'' is by hypothesis negative) is given by the equations $kf'(y_1) = c$, $kf'(y_2) = c$, $kf'(y_3) = c$
> Therefore y_1, y_2, &c, are all equal: the law of distribution is equality. (1877, p. 43)

Here the Lagrange multiplier is denoted by c, but no definition is given by Edgeworth, who then immediately considers the cases where both β and k vary among individuals, stating that, 'Unto him that hath greater capacity for pleasure shall be added more of the means of pleasure' (1877, p. 43). Further complexities are then examined using the same basic approach. Edgeworth wished to emphasize that utilitarianism only implies equality of the 'means of pleasure' under the special set of assumptions described above, and in the general case the prescribed solution will be some form of inequality. He also extended his analysis to deal with the distribution of effort, as well as 'rewards', arguing not surprisingly that most work should be provided by those most capable of providing it. A yet more general treatment of the problem was allowed with the use of the calculus of variations, but again Edgeworth provided the reader with virtually no help in following his mathematical argument.

What is noticeable about Edgeworth's first published mathematics, involving the use of Lagrangian methods, and the calculus of variations for some general problems, is that he made no attempt to explain his method to the reader. As seen at the beginning of section 2.3 below, these methods were well beyond the vast majority of contemporary philosophers and economists. It is really not surprising that few of Edgeworth's contributions formed the basis for continuous development. Even by the standards of the late nineteenth century Edgeworth's range was remarkable, and it is so unfortunate that he did not make a much greater effort to improve the clarity of his exposition. Despite later appeals, by, for example, the very sympathetic Jevons, Edgeworth never managed to produce a style of exposition that made his work more widely accessible. Indeed, he often seemed to take the view that since the analysis *is* very difficult and will anyway only be understood by a few people, there is no point in making concessions to the reader. Other explanations are of course possible.

Edgeworth's analysis of the utilitarian optimal distribution was continued in his paper on 'The hedonical calculus' (1879), which was later reprinted as the third part of *Mathematical Psychics*. Discussion of this is therefore best delayed until chapter 5.

2.3 Early Technical Contributions

Walras, Jevons and Lagrange Multipliers

The fact that, as seen above, the *New and Old Methods of Ethics* contained extensive use of Lagrangian methods and the calculus of variations seems to have been overlooked in the literature. Jaffé (1964, 1977) has discussed a letter to Walras from Herman Amstein in 1877, who carefully explained how a problem posed by Walras could be answered using Lagrangian methods. Jaffé wrote that, 'Had Walras's competence in mathematics been adequate to the task . . . he would have introduced . . . into the *Elements* as early as 1877 a momentous technical innovation which did not take firm root in the literature of mathematical economics until the following century' (1977, p. 202). When the letter was reprinted by Baumol and Goldfeld (1968, p. 189) they suggested that, although the Amstein letter was earlier, the first publication containing Lagrange multipliers was Edgeworth's *Mathematical Psychics* of 1881. This view is acknowledged, and repeated, by Jaffé (1977, p. 203, n. 21).

It is interesting to note that Jevons also received a letter which explained how the differential calculus could be used in the analysis of the use of several factors in production, and in constrained utility maximization. The letter, from Harald Westergaard in 1878, has now been published in Black (1977a, pp. 254–8). Nevertheless it was mentioned by Jevons in the preface to the 1879 second edition of his *Theory of Political Economy*, where he said that, 'the whole question is one of maxima and minima, the mathematical conditions of which are familiar to mathematicians', but that he preferred to use his more laborious presentation for 'readers who, like myself, are not skilful and professional mathematicians' (1957, pp. xii–xiii). Thus Jevons, like Walras, was unable to make much use of the advice from more highly trained mathematicians. Thus two of the most original economists of the last century, who vigorously advocated the application of mathematics to their subject, did not master this method or chose not to use it for purposes of exposition.

Multiple Solutions

In using Lagrange multipliers in 1877, Edgeworth was also careful to discuss possible complications. First he referred to the possibility of multiple solutions, and after examining second-order conditions, he wrote:

> It is not pretended that even the mathematical reasoning of the preceding theory is free from objection. Thus, it might be objected that account is taken only of *some* solutions of the system of equations. (1877, p. 48–9)

The discussion of multiple solutions was further amplified by several rather fanciful examples of a snake climbing a mountain (1877, p. 48), and where the utility functions, 'consisted of two billows swelling concavely . . . and separated by a convex trough' (1877, p. 62). Multiple solutions were also discussed in *Mathematical Psychics*, (1881, pp. 68, n. 3; 92).

Of greater interest is his recognition of the problem of solving for y from the implicit functions which are obtained by setting the first derivatives of the Lagrangian equal to zero. He states:

> Again, it may be objected that the equation $kf'(y) = c$ may afford more than one available value for y . . . But since $(d_2\pi/dy^2)$ is continually negative, it is evident that a certain value of $(d\pi/dy)$ produced by a certain value of y, can never be reproduced by any other value of y. It might be otherwise, if the condition $(d_2\pi/dy^2)$ to be negative were even slightly infringed. (1877, p. 49–50)

This is in fact a corollary of the condition required by what would now be called the 'implicit function theorem'. It may also be noted that although Edgeworth (1881, pp. 26–7) seems also to have been the first person to use determinants in economics (see the next chapter and also Baumol and Goldfeld, 1968, p. 189), he did not use them when discussing second-order conditions for constrained maximization. He did not extend his discussion to consideration of the problem of solving a set of implicit functions for several variables, where the implicit function theorem requires that the Jacobian should be non-zero.

Corner Solutions and Inequality Constraints

Edgeworth also explicitly discussed corner solutions and inequality constraints at an earlier date than is sometimes suggested. In their introduction to the reprint of Edgeworth's paper on 'Monopoly' (published in Italian in 1897, and in English in 1925) Baumol and Goldfeld refer to his substitution of an, 'inequality for an equality constraint – perhaps for the first time in the literature' (1968, p. 190). Nevertheless, they note (1968, p. 168, n. 7) that Walras discussed corner solutions in the *Elements* (1874, lesson 9). Walras's discussion was in the context of the equality of the price ratio with the ratio of marginal utilities. Furthermore Westergaard explicitly mentions corner solutions in his letter to Jevons (see Black, 1977a, p. 256).

However, Edgeworth clearly mentioned their importance as early as 1881 when he said:

> It is not universally necessary that the first term of variation should vanish. It suffices for a maximum that the *first term* of variation should be known to be negative . . . Such knowledge is generally the result of *imposed conditions* . . . that a curve must not pass outside a given boundary, must not exclude a given point, must be convex. It is submitted that such complicating imposed conditions have some analogy with the conditions imposed by necessity upon practical politics and applied utilitarianism (1881, p. 93).

Edgeworth's work is indeed remarkable for the extent to which he used advanced mathematics to make significant progress in economics. Further contributions will be mentioned in later chapters. In view of these important innovations it is interesting that he does not seem to have had a formal training in advanced mathematics. Samuelson refers to him as a 'self-taught barrister' (1974, p. 1279, n. 1), Bowley refers to his 'want of systematic training' (1934, p. 114), and Edgeworth himself said that the theory 'could be presented by a professed mathematician more elegantly and scientifically' (1881, p. 24).

The lack of training is evident in his writing. For example, Baumol and Goldfeld refer to his 'nearly unreadable mathematical exposition' (1968, p. 189), and Keynes says that he was 'clumsy and awkward' (1972, p. 256). When discussing Edgeworth's mathematics, Kendall suggests that, 'It would . . . be of considerable interest if we could discover how and when Edgeworth acquired his mathematics, and under what incentive' (1970, p. 258). It is this question which is considered in the following section.

2.4 Edgeworth's Mathematical Training

The paucity of direct information about Edgeworth's life makes it unlikely that Kendall's question about his mathematical training can ever be answered with certainty. However, there are a number of connections which have not previously been indicated in studies of Edgeworth, the most important of them being with W. R. Hamilton and W. K. Clifford. It has been suggested (by Eisenhart in discussion of Stigler, 1978, p. 319) that Sir Francis Beaufort (1774–1857) may have been influential, because of the friendship and complex family relationship between Beaufort and the Edgeworths. However, it is unlikely that his mathematics were sufficiently advanced. Furthermore, he died when Edgeworth was only 12 years old.

Trinity College Dublin

The possibility that Edgeworth may have been exposed to serious mathematics at Trinity College Dublin, despite the fact that his main training was in the classics and literature, is worth considering. No records are available, although Bowley suggested that when Edgeworth entered Trinity in 1862, 'it may be presumed he studied both mathematics and classics' (1934, p. 113). In this connection it is of interest that a tutor of Edgeworth at Trinity was J. K. Ingram (1823–1907), but although Ingram initially showed promise as a mathematician he later regretted the time spent on mathematics, was strongly averse to its application in economics, and had little sympathy with a priori reasoning.

Of greater relevance is the fact that Trinity College Dublin had an excellent curriculum in mathematics. This was largely the result of efforts by Rev. Bartholomew Lloyd who was Professor of Mathematics, Natural Philosophy, Greek and Divinity at Trinity, and later became Provost of the college and President of the Royal Irish Academy. Lloyd instituted a revolution in mathematics teaching after 1812, when he introduced French textbooks into the college and had other texts written in order to teach the work of the continental mathematicians. His son Humphrey Lloyd (1800–81) became Vice-Provost of Trinity in 1862, the year in which Edgeworth entered. There are several further points worth noting in relation to other possible sources. Humphrey Lloyd's first research, in optics, was directly stimulated by a question from William Rowan Hamilton (whose possible role is discussed further below); and he was later involved with much work on terrestrial magnetism. It may not be coincidental that Edgeworth (1881, pp. 13–14) presented a complex analogy involving electro-magnetic fields.

Family Influences

Despite the strong scientific and literary interests of the large Edgeworth family, there seems to be no clear evidence concerning his mathematical training. However, it is known that although Edgeworth's father Francis Beaufort Edgeworth (1809–46) hated mathematics, he was a close friend of Sir William Rowan Hamilton (1805–65). Hamilton kept in touch with Edgeworth's mother after F. B. Edgeworth's death, and spent most of his life at the Dunsink Observatory near Dublin. He did important and original work in the calculus of variations and in his theory of biquaternions. In view of Edgeworth's eulogistic remarks about Lagrange in *Mathematical Psychics* it is worth noting Hamilton's comment on the *Mécanique Analytique*, that it could only be described as 'a scientific poem' (see Ball, 1924, p. 408). The beauty of Lagrange's work was that everything was deduced, using the calculus of variations, from a single principle (the principle of least action). When Edgeworth referred to Hamilton in *Mathematical Psychics* he was talking of the use of utilitarianism as the 'one central idea' (1881, p. 94). Hamilton's work was characterized by a high degree of abstraction and generality, which made it difficult to read and meant that, like Edgeworth's work, it was some time before its value was fully recognized.

A second family connection concerns the Rev. Thomas Romney Robinson (1792–1882), astronomer and mathematical physicist. He was, from 1823, in charge of the Armagh observatory, and his publications include work on electricity, magnetism, heat, and mechanics, in addition to astronomy. Robinson's second wife was Lucy Jane Edgeworth (1805–97), an aunt of Edgeworth, and Robinson was a frequent guest at Edgeworthstown.

Robinson also provides an additional family connection, through his daughter, Mary Suzanna Robinson (d. 1899). In 1857 she married Sir George Gabriel Stokes (1819–1903), Lucasian Professor of mathematics at Cambridge from 1849 until his death. Stokes was a close friend of William Thomson (Lord Kelvin). Both Stokes and Kelvin are mentioned in *Mathematical Psychics*, but there seems to be no direct evidence relating to the extent of any contact between Edgeworth and Stokes. Stokes's successor as Lucasian Professor was Joseph Larmor (1857–1942). Larmor edited Stokes's scientific correspondence, was a champion of Lagrange's 'principle of least action', and was known to have admired Edgeworth's mathematics (see Price, 1946, p. 41).

Other Connections

It is clear that Edgeworth's family background was sufficient to stimulate scientific and mathematical interest, in addition to his classical and literary interests. But a clue to a further connection which should be mentioned is provided by the psychologist James Sully, mentioned earlier in section 2.1. In his autobiography Sully discusses his association with the Savile Club, and says, 'It was the same sociable club which introduced me to W. K. Clifford, the brilliant young mathematician and thinker; to F. Y. Edgeworth . . . as well as to other lovers of ideas' (1918, p. 164). Edgeworth's membership of the Savile was also mentioned by Bowley (1934, p. 122), Keynes (1972, p. 266) and Price (1946, p. 38). Sully was elected to the Savile in 1875. There are no records of Edgeworth's election, but in 1872 he proposed his brother Antonio for membership. One of the seconders was Alfred Graves, a friend from Trinity College Dublin (see Graves, 1931, p. 129) and a nephew of R. P. Graves, the author of *The Life of William Rowan Hamilton* (1882). This book gives many examples of the close connection between Hamilton and the Edgeworth family, and was mentioned by F. Y. Edgeworth (1925, ii, p. 289, n. 3). William Kingdon Clifford (1845–79) was not only a brilliant mathematician, but had wide interests in literature and philosophy. He had worked on the theory of biquaternions, and on the mechanics of fluids and gases, and was an effective teacher. For example, Ball (1924, p. 491, n. 1) says that, 'His remarkable felicity of illustration and power of seizing analogies made him one of the most brilliant expounders of mathematical principles.' Indeed in the *New and Old Methods of Ethics*, Edgeworth, when referring to evolution, mentions 'one of the ablest expositors of such a system, Professor Clifford' (1877, p. 87). In discussing non-Euclidean geometry he also said, 'it is rather as if the geometrical circumstances of our ancestors had differed from ours; so that our inheritance of axioms should relate to those worlds, of which Professor Clifford tells us, where the shortest line is *not* a straight line' (1877, p. 13). While there seems to be no direct evidence, it is therefore quite possible that he knew and was influenced by Clifford.

Edgeworth provides a further example of someone who made original use of mathematical techniques in economics, after learning the techniques for a different reason. It seems that most progress has been made in this way, rather than by economists who, having formulated a problem, call on mathematicians for help. For example, it has been seen that even Walras and Jevons were unable to use advice from skilled mathematicians. Of course, mathematical ability is not sufficient to guarantee significant progress, as, for example, in the case of Whewell. Other economists who may be compared with Edgeworth in this respect include Fisher, Pareto and later Hotelling (along with others in the United States who will be discussed in chapter 8). Their contributions must also be distinguished from those of mathematical economists who use technique for its own sake. Similarly, it should be no surprise that important, if sporadic, contributions to economics have been made by engineers such as Antonelli, Dupuit, Ellet, Isnard and Launhardt, whose work led them towards genuine economic problems connected with transport.

Further Reading

Joseph Priestley was a later member of the Lunar Society of Birmingham (see Schofield, 1963), and was well known to Edgeworth's grandfather. Maria Edgeworth's contacts with continental utilitarians is evident from the letters edited by Colvin (1979). F. H. Bradley was the leading British Idealist; his criticism of Sidgwick is in *Mind* (1877). Also of importance is Bradley (1876); for further discussion see Schneewind (1977). It has been noted above that German idealism had a much stronger influence on the thought of Marshall. Brief notes on the psychologists mentioned by Edgeworth may be found in the appendix to this book. For a discussion of the views of George Cornewall Lewis and John Austin on authority, and their influence on J. S. Mill, see Friedman (1969). Both are mentioned in *Mathematical Psychics*; see the appendix.

Edgeworth's views on authority may be contrasted with those of Jevons (for example his famous comment on the 'noxious influence of authority'). However, Jevons was prepared to argue that his discovery of precursors, and independent works such as that of Walras, provided evidence of the 'correctness' of his views.

Edgeworth was, as noted above and shown in the next chapter, an early user of determinants in economics; on their use by Antonelli and Pareto, see Baumol and Goldfeld (1968). For Keynes's view of the contrast between Marshall and Edgeworth as mathematicians, see Keynes (1972, p. 256). Concerning the possible influence of Sir Francis Beaufort on Edgeworth's mathematics, it is also worth noting that there is no mention of Edgeworth in the detailed biography by Friendly (1977), which nevertheless contains much discussion of the Edgeworth family. Richard Lovell Edgeworth's fourth wife was Beaufort's eldest sister Frances Anne (1769–1865), and Beaufort's second wife was Honora Edgeworth (1897–1957), a daughter of Richard Lovell Edgeworth by his third wife. Thomas Romney Robinson's daughter Mary Suzanna was in fact a daughter by Robinson's first marriage, to Eliza Isabelle Rambaut (d. 1837). The family relationship with Galton should not be forgotten, but there does not seem to have been much direct contact, and Edgeworth is not mentioned by Galton's biographer Forrest (1974), nor by Galton (1908). However, Galton attempted to get Edgeworth elected to the Royal Society in 1889, 1894 and 1896. Ingram's views on methodology were clearly stated (1878, 1893); see also the notes to chapter 3. Sir William Rowan Hamilton's work on 'biquaternions' involved abandoning the commutative laws of algebra and led to further work in matrix theory. P. G. Tait (mentioned several times in *Mathematical Psychics*; see the appendix) was one of Hamilton's supporters; they were in correspondence from 1858 (see also Tait, 1867). Hamilton's very close contact with the Edgeworth family is clearly shown in the biography by R. P. Graves (1882). His work on biquaternions was for long thought to have few practical uses, but the later related work of H. G. Grassman (for some time neglected) has led to important results. Unfortunately it is not known whether the Balliol mathematician H. J. S. Smith (1826–83) had any influence, although Smith and Jowett (Edgeworth's tutor) held joint parties, and Smith was a great friend of W. K. Clifford. For further details of Clifford's work see the introduction to his *Lectures and Essays* (1879). Clifford was at University College London, where Jevons was appointed in 1875, and in a lecture of 1877 Clifford took Jevons's work as his point of departure (see Clifford, *Papers*, 1882, pp. 1–16). He was also a member of the Grote Club, which included Marshall (see also Keynes, 1972, pp. 167, 174, n. 3). On Edgeworth's early mathematics, see also Creedy (1980b, 1983).

3

The Economical Calculus

The previous chapter concentrated on a number of neglected aspects of Edgeworth's early work on utilitarianism. His most substantial original contribution was the mathematical analysis of the distributive implications of maximizing total utility, subject to a fixed amount of resources, and where utility functions were allowed to vary over time and among individuals. Utilitarianism was being used as a principle of distributive justice, involving direct comparisons among individuals.

There is no evidence that Edgeworth had any interest in economics at this time; indeed it seems that he was ignorant of the work of Jevons and Marshall until 1879. In *Mathematical Psychics*, Edgeworth added a note stating that his paper of 1879 in *Mind* was offered, 'without acknowledgement, because without knowledge, of the cumulative proofs already adduced by Prof. Jevons' (1881, p. 34, n. 1). Edgeworth stated quite clearly that his first knowledge of Marshall came from Jevons who, 'highly praised the then recently published *Economics of Industry*' (in Pigou, ed, 1925b, p. 66). This book could not have been seen by Jevons until late in 1879, since in a letter from Marshall to Jevons (dated 30 June 1879) he says that the *Economics of Industry* is 'nearly finished' and 'one of the first bound copies will find its way to Hampstead' (see Pigou, ed, 1925b, p. 371).

It seems that Edgeworth was introduced to Jevons by Sully in 1879. Sully moved to Hampstead, where Edgeworth had lodgings in Mount Vernon and where Jevons also lived, in 1878 (see Sully, 1918, pp. 180, 223). It is the contact with Jevons which produced the turning point in Edgeworth's work. Section 3.1 shows how Edgeworth became interested in the problem of the indeterminacy of the rate of exchange, arising from the existence of only a small number of transactors. This led directly to Edgeworth's second book, *Mathematical Psychics* (1881), which marked a crucial stage in his career, and which was clearly written in a state of considerable enthusiasm for his new subject. The nature of the book and its approach to economics are examined in section 3.2. Edgeworth's own highly original analysis of the problem of barter, involving his indifference curves and the contract curve, is then discussed in section 3.3. This describes Edgeworth's framework for his remarkable analysis of the way in which competition among a large number of traders reduces the range of indeterminacy, which is the subject of chapter 4.

3.1 Indeterminacy in Exchange

Jevons's work in the *Theory of Political Economy*, of which Edgeworth remained ignorant until 1879, involved the application of very basic mathematics, and of psychological research, to the analysis of exchange in competitive markets. Edgeworth's belated contact with Jevons proved to be crucial for several reasons. First there was the direct stimulus provided by the *Theory of Political Economy*, and by an anonymous review of Jevons's book in the *Saturday Review* (1871). Secondly, it was Jevons who introduced Edgeworth to the work of Marshall. These factors are discussed in turn below. Some indication of Edgeworth's personal regard for Jevons can be obtained from a letter to Mrs Jevons after the death of her husband in 1882. He wrote: 'I shall always remember with gratitude the kind encouragement and a peculiar intellectual sympathy which he extended to one whose studies were in the same direction, however immeasurably behind his', and, 'I shall always regard it as one of the privileges of my life to have come under the influence of his serene and lofty intellect' (see Black, 1962, p. 202).

Jevons and Price Determination

The crucial development following Edgeworth's contact with Jevons was not simply the realization that mathematics could be used to examine equilibrium in exchange. Rather it was that in his analysis Jevons explicitly assumed, through his 'law of indifference', that all individuals take the equilibrium prices as given. In using this law as 'one of the central pivots of the theory', Jevons stated that, 'there can only be one ratio of exchange of one uniform commodity at any moment' (1957, p. 87). This uniformity was implicitly achieved by arbitrage. In Jevons's model, price taking was axiomatic, and his theory was explicitly limited to the static equilibrium conditions. As he suggested: 'it is a far more easy task to lay down the conditions under which trade is completed and interchange ceases, than to attempt to ascertain at which rate trade will go when equilibrium is not attained' (1957, p. 94). Jevons was concerned with the properties of the price-taking equilibrium, and deliberately excluded the role of the number of competitors from his analysis via the rather awkward notion of the 'trading body', discussed further in chapter 4.

In a section on 'Failure of the Laws of Exchange', Jevons discussed cases in which some indeterminacy would result. His most notable example was of house sales, where it was suggested that indeterminacy would result from the discrete nature of the good being exchanged. While the major part of the *Saturday Review* article concentrated on attacking Jevons's use of mathematics, 'to wrap up a plain statement in a mysterious collection of letters', the reviewer also took exception to the discussion of house sales. He suggested that Jevons 'thinks, however, that the difficulty is owing to the fact that the house cannot be sold by separate bricks, whereas it is really owing in our opinion to the assumed absence of competition' (see Black, 1981, p. 157). In view of the relevance of this review, it is of interest to find that Jevons himself took it seriously, and indeed rated it higher than Marshall's review in the *Academy*. In 1874 he wrote to a correspondent (J. D'Aulnis) that, 'As to the reviews in the English periodical journals, that in the *Saturday Review* of 11th November 1871 is the most important, and indeed the only one requiring any attention. There was indeed a review in the *Academy* of 1st April 1872, but though more fair than that of the *Saturday Review*, it contained no criticism worthy of your notice' (see Black, 1977b, p. 62). It seems likely that Jevons mentioned the review to Edgeworth.

It is interesting that the question of the number of traders and indeterminacy was also raised directly with Jevons in a letter from R. O. Williams in 1875. He wrote, 'I would say that the difficulty . . . was in the restricted conditions of the market rather than in the indivisibility of one of the subjects of exchange' (see Black, 1977b, pp. 153–4). Of even more importance is the fact that Jevons had corresponded with Fleeming Jenkin (1833–85), who raised the question of indeterminacy with just two traders who were not price takers, even before completion of the *Theory of Political Economy*. The correspondence with Jenkin arose from the publication of the latter's paper on 'Trade Unions: How Far Legitimate' in 1868 (Jenkin, 1931), in which he used mathematics. Jenkin sent the paper to Jevons, who in reply sent a copy of his own paper which he read to the British Association in 1862. The highly revealing letters from Jenkin (in Black, 1977a, pp. 166–78) devote a great deal of attention to the case of exchange between two persons. The basic difference between them was that Jevons, as in the later *Theory of Political Economy*, explicitly assumed price-taking behaviour, whereas Jenkin examined barter. He could not see why two *isolated* individuals should accept the price-taking equilibrium, whereas Jevons was considering the behaviour of two *typical* individuals in a large market. The following extract from a letter from Jenkin is particularly relevant:

> There is no motive operating on their minds to induce them to agree on this rate [of exchange]. Jones would like more cotton for his silk, Brown would like more silk for his cotton and I do not see how any considerations as to the rate at which their desires fluctuate with the quantity can determine their desire for any one quantity. This must it seems to me be determined by wholly different considerations. You appear to me to assume that the ratio of exchange would be that fixed by the intersection of the curves . . . but in order that this should be true it would be necessary that the aggregate utilities to *each* party should increase up to that point which is not true. (Black, 1977a, p. 177)

The correspondence with Jenkin is quite one-sided, however, and Jevons's reaction to these points is not known. It must of course be remembered that the relationship between Jenkin and Jevons was complicated by the fact that it was Jenkin's paper on 'The graphic representation of the laws of supply and demand' in 1870 that stimulated Jevons to publish his own work more quickly in book form, in order to establish priority (see Black, 1970, p. 14).

It was this gap in Jevons's analysis which Edgeworth set out to fill, and he makes particular mention of the *Saturday Review* in *Mathematical Psychics*; in fact, no other reviews of the *Theory of Political Economy* were mentioned. Edgeworth's objective was to introduce explicitly the role of the number of traders into the analysis of competitive markets. His achievement in this respect was to show the conditions under which competition between buyers and sellers, through a barter process, would lead to a final settlement which is in fact equivalent to one in which all individuals act independently as price takers. As he later stated (1925, ii, p. 453), 'the existence of a uniform rate of exchange between any two commodities is perhaps not so much axiomatic as deducible from the process of competition in a perfect market'. How he achieved this will be explained in chapter 4; the present chapter concentrates on the basic framework, which Edgeworth introduced very quickly as he was impatient to move to the more substantial analysis of the effects of competition among traders. It is ironic that most basic economic textbooks now concentrate mainly on this framework, to the neglect of the analysis of the role of the number of competitors. There was, however, a further influence on Edgeworth's early concentration on indeterminacy in the rate of exchange, which must now be discussed.

Marshall and Wage Bargaining

It has been shown that Jevons also introduced Edgeworth to Marshall's published work. The influence of Marshall's *The Pure Theory of Foreign Trade. The Pure Theory of Domestic Values* (1879) is clear; Edgeworth later said that on first seeing Marshall's work he, 'discerned a new power of mathematical reasoning' (see Pigou, 1925b, p. 66). It will be seen that in 1881 he provided the basic analytics, in terms of indifference curves, of Marshall's reciprocal demand curves. But more importantly for the present discussion, Marshall seems to have led Edgeworth to the subject of indeterminacy in wage bargaining. The clue to this is found in Edgeworth's reference in *Mathematical Psychics* (1881, p. 48, n. 1) to Thornton's comparison of the determination of prices in Dutch and English auctions. He gave no bibliographical reference to Thornton, and it seems most likely that Edgeworth obtained this reference from a footnote in Alfred and Mary Paley Marshall's joint book on the *Economics of Industry* (1879). This note states: 'If there are very few buyers in a market, it may make a great difference whether goods are sold by Dutch or English auctions . . . See Thornton *On Labour*, 2nd ed. pp. 56, 7' (1879, p. 200, n. 1). It is also significant that this footnote was placed in a chapter on the 'Influence of Trade Unions on Wages', where the Marshalls suggest that trade unions may secure for workers a larger share of the wages-and-profits Fund. Thus:

> If the labourers throughout a country have been in the habit of selling their labour without reserve, they may have received

> among them a smaller share of the Wages-and-Profit Fund than they would have got if there had been perfectly free competition among employers, or than they would have got if they had been able to offer their labour at a reserve price . . . If then the labourers enter into local trade combinations, and refuse to sell their labour except at a reserve price, it is quite possible that they may increase their share of the Wages-and-Profits Fund, and raise wages at the expense of profits. (1879, p. 200)

It is worth pointing out that Marshall later rejected this first edition, and after 1890 subsequent editions of the *Economics of Industry* were issued under Alfred Marshall's name only, and consisted of basic material abstracted from his *Principles of Economics*. Because of Edgeworth's familiarity with the Marshalls' book it seems very likely that their discussion of indeterminacy in the context of wage bargaining had a direct influence on Edgeworth's work.

It is, however, worth pointing out that he could also have been made aware of Thornton's discussion of Dutch and English auctions by reading Jevons's *Theory of Political Economy* (1957, pp. 108–9). Jevons (1957, p. 123) actually quoted Thornton's discussion of indeterminacy before giving his own example of house sales. The common reference of Marshall and Jevons to Thornton is to his book *On Labour: Its Wrongful Claims and Rightful Dues* (1869), and it was the same book which led to J. S. Mill's famous rejection of the wages-fund theory. When mentioning indeterminacy in the context of auctions, Edgeworth actually comments: 'As Thornton suggests. Now we believe, but not because that un-mathematical writer has told us' (1881, p. 48, n. 1). This rather less than generous comment on Thornton may perhaps be explained by the fact that Jevons dismissed other aspects of Thornton's work. Jevons objected to Thornton's argument that, because of the existence of various exceptions, there are no regular laws of supply and demand. He concluded that, 'most of Mr. Thornton's arguments are beside the question' (1957, p. 108).

These discussions of indeterminacy, arising from the small number of competitors on each side of the market, seem to have provided an important stimulus for Edgeworth to examine explicitly the role of the number of competitors in the formation of the exchange rate. The example, mentioned by the Marshalls, of the role of combinations of labour in reducing the number of competitors and increasing the range of indeterminacy in contract was considered at length by Edgeworth.

While discussing these influences on Edgeworth's early work it is worth mentioning that Jevons, despite his extensive bibliographical researches, had no knowledge of Menger's work. Although Menger had considered indeterminacy in the rate of exchange, or 'price conflict', this was largely associated with imperfections other than that of the limitation of the number of traders, such as imperfect knowledge and quality differences (see, for example, Streissler, 1972). There is therefore no mention of Menger in *Mathematical Psychics*, but he was discussed briefly in the *Papers* (1925, ii, p. 307) when Edgeworth disagreed with his 'equal division solution' to indeterminacy. Other analyses of barter and indeterminacy will be discussed at the end of chapter 4.

3.2 Mathematical Psychics

Edgeworth was 36 years old when *Mathematical Psychics: An Essay on the Application of Mathematics to the Moral Sciences* was published in 1881. The slim volume of 150 pages marked his first contribution to what would now be referred to as 'mainstream' economic literature, although of course the boundaries between subjects were not then so firmly drawn. This highly original monograph was well received by a very small group of 'experts', but was for many years neglected, so that it was not until the middle of the present century that many of its central ideas began to be more fully appreciated. A large part of this neglect of such important analytical contributions must be attributed to the style of the book and to the character of the author.

Reviews of the Book

Edgeworth was extremely fortunate in his reviewers. Substantial and sympathetic reviews appeared in *Mind* and the *Academy* by Jevons and Marshall respectively. It was Marshall's second and last book review, his first being of Jevons's *Theory of Political Economy*, and it began, 'This book shows clear signs of genius, and is a promise of great things to come' (1881, rep. 1975, p. 265). Jevons began by stating that 'whatever else readers of this book may think about it, they would probably all agree that it is a very remarkable one' (1881, p. 581). It is not surprising, in view of the discussion of the previous section above, that in noting Edgeworth's analysis of wage bargaining Marshall commented that, 'this is, of course, not entirely new, but it is put in a new way' (1881, rep. 1975, p. 267). Furthermore Marshall argued, in contrast to the position taken by Edgeworth, that, 'the greater part of economic theory can be dealt with most easily' by the use of supply and demand curves rather than by the analysis of barter on which Edgeworth had concentrated. This position was to be argued at much greater length in his *Principles of Economics* (1890), and is discussed in chapter 6 below.

Both Jevons and Marshall agreed about the style of the book. Marshall's view, considering the gestation period of his *Principles*, was somewhat restrained:

> His readers may sometimes wish that he had kept his work by him a little longer till he had worked it out more fully, and obtained that simplicity which comes only through long labour. But, taking it at what it claims to be, 'a tentative study', we can only admire its brilliance, force, and originality. (1881, rep. 1975, p. 267)

Jevons referred to the book as 'an uncouth and even clumsy piece of literary work', with a style that, 'if not obscure, is *implicit*, so that the reader is left to puzzle out every important sentence like an enigma' (1881, p. 583). Jevons made the interesting point that readers in the social sciences would not make the required effort, although they would if 'some great pecuniary matter like a great lawsuit' depended on it. His statement that, 'The book is one of the most difficult to read which we ever came across, certainly the most difficult of those purporting to treat of economic science' (1881, p. 581) was echoed 76 years later by Stigler. He wrote that, 'few economists of his time or ours have attempted to disentangle and uncover the theorems and conjectures of the *Mathematical Psychics*, probably the most elusively written book of importance in the history of economics' (1957, reprinted in 1965, p. 246).

After seeing Jevons's review, Galton wrote an encouraging letter to Edgeworth in which he stated that he was 'totally at issue' with Jevons's view (see Stigler, 1978, p. 246). Edgeworth obviously showed this letter to Jevons, who, in a rare letter between the two close neighbours, stressed that, 'I have your success quite as much at heart as Mr. Galton', and again stressed the importance of clear writing. His wise advice, that, 'by plenty of care and practice you may attain lucidity and skill in writing and I am sure it is essential to success as an author' seems unfortunately to have had little impact on Edgeworth's subsequent work. As argued in chapter 1, his easy access to publication, first by self-financing his books and then as editor of the *Economic Journal*, failed to impose the necessary constraints on his style. Too little is known about Edgeworth's personality to warrant further speculation about this failure to communicate more widely, although some sign of contempt for a wider readership is indicated in his later review of the third edition of Marshall's *Principles* (1895). He commented that

> A feeling of relief and satisfaction may be experienced by another sort of susceptible *doctrinaire* when the *doyen* of English economists appears in a literary garb which can excite no suspicion of his being tainted with a form of error much condemned by those who have no mind to it – the inordinate use of reasoning. (1925, iii, p. 64)

It was suggested by Keynes (1972, p. 255) that Marshall's review in the *Academy* led to the friendship between Marshall and Edgeworth. But in fact this began earlier, after Edgeworth sent Marshall a copy of his *New and Old Methods of Ethics*. A letter from Marshall, dated 8 Feb. 1880, began: 'I have now read nearly all the book you sent us, and am extremely delighted by many things in it. There seems to be a very close agreement between us as to the promise of mathematics in the sciences that relate to man's actions'. He very quickly retracted the rather strong last statement, and in a letter to Edgeworth of 28 March 1880 wrote, 'I intend never to use analysis when I can use geometry'.

Unnumerical Mathematics

After a brief 'introductory description of contents' (there was no contents page), Part 1 of *Mathematical Psychics* (1881, pp. 1–15) was devoted mainly to a justification of the use of mathematics in economics where precise data are not available. Edgeworth's use of mathematics has been discussed briefly in chapter 1, and many of his arguments will now be familiar to the modern reader, but in such a pioneering study he was obliged to justify his approach at length. Furthermore, there is probably no other apology in the whole of economic literature which compares with Edgeworth's passionate plea for the application of mathematics. For example, when considering individual utility maximization, and the point that it is not necessary to have precise absolute measures of utility, he says:

> *Atoms of pleasure* are not easy to distinguish and discern; more continuous than sand, more discrete than liquid; as it were nuclei of the just-perceivable, embedded in circumambient semi-consciousness.
>
> We cannot *count* the golden sands of life; we cannot *number* the 'innumerable smile' of seas of love; but we seem to be capable of observing that there is here a *greater*, there a *less*, multitude of pleasure-units; mass of happiness; and that is enough. (1881, pp. 8–9)

Great stress was placed on comparison with the physical sciences, and especially with the role of Lagrange's 'Principle of least action' in examining the overall effects produced by the interactions among many particles. The connection with Edgeworth's analysis of competition, involving interaction among a large number of competitors to produce a determinate rate of exchange, is central here. The attraction of the fact that in the natural sciences so much could be derived from a single principle was very strong for both Jevons and Edgeworth. But Edgeworth took this to its ultimate limit in arguing that the comparable single principle in social sciences, that of maximum utility, would produce results of comparable value. Referring to Laplace's massive work entitled *Mécanique Céleste* (published in parts between 1799 and 1825), he suggested that:

> 'Mécanique Sociale' may one day take her place along with 'Mécanique Céleste', throned each upon the double-sided height of one maximum principle, the supreme pinnacle of moral as of physical science . . . the movements of each soul, whether selfishly isolated or linked sympathetically, may continually be realising the maximum energy of pleasure, the Divine love of the universe. (1881, p. 12)

The point Edgeworth makes in saying that the 'souls' may be selfishly isolated or linked sympathetically is essentially an allusion to his later results in *Mathematical Psychics*. These results concern the 'recontracting process' which allows for co-operative behaviour, the result that the competitive solution is on the contract curve, and that the utilitarian arrangement is on the contract curve (with the introduction of 'sympathy' having no significant effect on the shape of the contract curve). These results will be examined in much more detail in chapters 4 and 5.

3.3 Exchange and Contract

Having argued that, '*the conception of Man as a pleasure machine* may justify and facilitate the employment of mechanical terms and Mathematical reasoning in social science' (1881, p. 15), Edgeworth then moved on to the analysis of the 'economical calculus', which formed the second part of *Mathematical Psychics*. The starting point of this division of 'the Calculus of Pleasure' is that, 'every agent is actuated only by self-interest' (1881, p. 16).

Economics is therefore concerned with examining the ultimate result arising from competition among 'jostling egoists', and Edgeworth compared this with Sidgwick's term 'Egoistic Hedonism'. In contrast, the 'Utilitarian Calculus', which formed the third part of *Mathematical Psychics*, and which is examined in chapter 5, is concerned with, 'the equilibrium of a system in which all tend to maximum universal utility' (1881, p. 15). He argued that between the two 'extremes' of egoism and pure utilitarianism, there is an infinite number of 'impure methods' where the utility of others 'counts for a fraction'. This aspect will also be discussed in chapter 5, but it is useful to recall here the discussion of chapter 2 and Edgeworth's earlier argument that egoism will tend towards utilitarianism in the course of evolution.

It is the modern restatement of Edgeworth's technical analysis of the 'economical calculus' for which he is best remembered. Thus Samuelson (1974, p. 1279) stated that, 'What is now seen to be magnificent about Edgeworth's *Mathematical Psychics* is his 40 pages of discussion on indifference contours, exchange, recontracting, supply and demand, contract curves and (deepest of all) the core'.

In modern analysis the 'analytical tools' invented by Edgeworth in 1881, such as the indifference map and the contract curve, are used in many different contexts. But they were not introduced by Edgeworth as techniques for their own sake. His purpose was to examine the nature of *barter* among individuals, rather than looking at the nature of equilibrium in the case where traders are all assumed to take prices as being fixed and outside their own control. He wanted to see if a determinate rate of exchange would be likely to result in barter situations where it is assumed only that individuals wish to maximize their own utility, considered solely as a function of their own consumption. With full knowledge of individuals' utility functions, and their initial endowments of goods, would it be possible to work out a 'determinate' rate of exchange at which trade would always take place? This is of course quite different from the problem of evaluating equilibrium price ratios for individuals who take prices as given; in a barter situation with few traders there is no reason why any individual should accept any rate of exchange as being outside his own control. Edgeworth's direct statement of the problem is worth reproducing.

> The PROBLEM to which attention is specially directed in this introductory summary is: *How far contract is indeterminate* – an inquiry of more than theoretical importance, if it show not only that indeterminateness tends to [be present] widely, but also in what direction an escape from its evils is to be sought. (1881, p. 20)

(The word 'prevent' was printed instead of 'be present', but this correction was noted by Edgeworth in his own copy, now deposited in the library of the London School of Economics.) The remainder of this chapter concentrates on Edgeworth's positing of the widespread existence of indeterminacy. His demonstration that such indeterminacy results fundamentally from the lack of independent competitors is examined in chapter 4. Even with a large number of individuals, as, for example, with many employers and employees in an industry, the increasing use of combinations (in the form of trade unions and employers' associations) would raise a great need for arbitration. Edgeworth's suggestion of a principle of arbitration which would, under certain conditions, be acceptable to all parties, will be discussed in chapter 5.

Indifference Curves and the Contract Curve

Edgeworth begins his analysis of the problem stated above by taking the simplest case of two individuals exchanging fixed quantities of two goods. The basic framework is that described by Jevons, where the first individual holds all of the initial stocks of the first good, and similarly for the second individual. He writes the utility functions of each individual, following Jevons's additive form, in terms of the amounts consumed after exchange (but does not bother to define the symbols used to denote initial stocks). The next paragraph then immediately defines the general utility function, the contract curve and indifference curves, in that order! His presentation can hardly be described as transparent.

The notation used by Edgeworth is not helpful; person X exchanges a quantity x of his good, and has utility $P = F(xy)$, while person Y has total utility $\Pi = \Phi(xy)$. In his review, Marshall (1881, rep. 1975, p. 266) correctly inserted the commas in the utility functions, to read $F(x, y)$ for example. But in the following discussion it seems useful to introduce an alternative system of notation. Thus consider individuals A and B trading in two goods X and Y. Person A starts with an amount a of good X, but no Y; while B begins with no X but with an amount b of good Y. The person A exchanges an amount x of good X for an amount y of good Y, and his total utility after exchange can be written as $U_A = U_A(x, y)$. The total utility of B is written as $U_B = U_B(x, y)$. The way in which U_A and U_B are expressed here requires further comment, since it seems to have confused some later critics (for example, Jaffé, 1974a). The modern approach would usually write the arguments of the utility function as the amounts *consumed* after exchange has taken place rather than, as in Edgeworth's case, the amounts *exchanged*. As Edgeworth was later to write, 'the two coordinates . . . represent the quantities of the two commodities exchanged, the *quid* and the *pro quo*' (1925, ii, p. 291), but he was extremely terse in 1881. There is in fact no need to write the longer form $U_A(a-x, y)$ and $U_B(x, b-y)$, because a and b are constants. In deriving the conditions for utility maximization, requiring partial derivatives, the two approaches give equivalent results so long as care is taken about the signs of the derivatives. In an appendix (1881, p. 105) Edgeworth actually found it more 'convenient' to write the utility function as (using the present notation) $U_A(-x, y)$. Edgeworth's approach is more natural given his emphasis on *exchange*, but the modern usage is usually in terms of demand analysis; that is, the allocation of a fixed money budget.

It should also be noted that this represents the first *use* of the general utility function where, 'utility is regarded as a function of the two variables, not the sum of two functions of each' (1881, p. 104). Edgeworth's earlier discussion of the need to use a general utility function, rather than the additive form, has already been examined in the previous chapter.

In the sentence which follows Edgeworth's introduction of the general utility function, he raised the question of the equilibrium which may be reached with, 'one or both refusing to move further'.

In barter the conditions of exchange must be reached by voluntary agreement, or *contract*, between the two parties, and of course it is fundamental that no egoist would agree to a contract which would make him worse off than before the exchange. The question thus concerns the nature of the *settlement* reached by two contracting parties. He immediately answered that 'contract' only supplies part of the answer so that, 'supplementary conditions . . . supplied by competition or ethical motives' will be required, and then wrote the equation of his famous contract curve (1881, pp. 20–1). He then presents three alternative, and all rather clumsy, derivations of the equation of the contract curve. The indifference curve, the 'line of indifference', is introduced in the course of the first derivation, although a diagram is not drawn until seven pages later. At the end of three pages Edgeworth, with much understatement, comments that, 'No doubt the one theory which has been thus differently expressed could be presented by a professed mathematician more elegantly and scientifically' (1881, p. 24).

Edgeworth considered the utility functions of the two individuals as plotted in a three dimensional graph, with total utility as the, 'ordinate drawn from any point on the plane xy (say the plane of the paper) to the surface' (1881, p. 21). The problem of obtaining the equilibrium values of x and y which, 'cannot be varied without the consent of the parties to it' was clearly stated as follows: 'It is required to find a point (xy) such that, *in whatever direction* we take an infinitely small step, [U_A] and [U_B] do not increase together, but that, while one increases, the other decreases' (1881, p. 21). The locus of such points, 'it is here proposed to call the *contract-curve*'. This is derived as follows. Consider first a movement for person A. The total derivative of U_A is given by

$$\mathrm{d}U_A = \frac{\partial U_A}{\partial x}\mathrm{d}x + \frac{\partial U_A}{\partial y}\mathrm{d}y \tag{3.1}$$

and, 'it is evident that [A] will step only on one side of a certain line, the *line of indifference*, as it might be called' (1881, p. 21). This is of course because A will only consider positive values of $\mathrm{d}U_A$; thus the equation of an indifference curve is

$$\frac{\partial U_A}{\partial x}\mathrm{d}x + \frac{\partial U_A}{\partial y}\mathrm{d}y = 0 \tag{3.2}$$

Edgeworth actually wrote the total derivative after transforming to polar coordinates (that is, he considered an individual moving a length ϱ along a line through the origin inclined at an angle of θ). In writing the equation of the indifference curve he then transformed back again and with no explanation wrote dx and dy as discrete changes. To obtain the contract curve Edgeworth then asked:

> If we enquire in what directions [A] and [B] will consent to move *together*, the answer is, in any direction between their respective lines of indifference, in a direction *positive* as it may be called *for both*. At what point then will they refuse to move at all? When their *lines* of *indifference* are coincident. (1881, p. 22)

Thus the slope of each individual's indifference curve, dx/dy, must be the same, and from (3.2) it can be seen that

$$\frac{-\mathrm{d}x}{\mathrm{d}y} = \frac{\partial U_{\mathrm{A}}}{\partial y} \bigg/ \frac{\partial U_{\mathrm{A}}}{\partial x} = \frac{\partial U_{\mathrm{B}}}{\partial y} \bigg/ \frac{\partial U_{\mathrm{B}}}{\partial x} \tag{3.3}$$

so that the equation of the contract curve is given by

$$\frac{\partial U_{\mathrm{A}}}{\partial x}\frac{\partial U_{\mathrm{B}}}{\partial y} - \frac{\partial U_{\mathrm{A}}}{\partial y}\frac{\partial U_{\mathrm{B}}}{\partial x} = 0 \tag{3.4}$$

Edgeworth's alternative derivations of the contract curve involved the movement, from an arbitrary position, along one person's indifference curve; 'motion is possible so long as, one party not losing, the other gains' (1881, p. 23). This is really the method now usually used to explain the concept in introductory economics courses, but Edgeworth used the Lagrange multiplier method: that is, of maximizing one person's utility subject to the condition that the other person's utility remains constant. He then generalized this approach further by considering movement from an initial position, by which both individuals gain, and specified an arbitrary function to determine the direction of movement. Edgeworth's own description is perhaps worth quoting as an example of his elusive style:

> The conditions being here (i) that the pleasure-energy of [A] and [B] considered each as a function of (certain values of)

the variables x and y should be functions of the *same* values: . . . that the charioteer-pleasures should drive their teams *together* over the plane of *xy*; (ii) that the joint-team should never be urged in a direction contrary to the *preference* of either individual; that the resultant line of force (and the momentum) of the gross, the chariot, system should be continually intermediate between the (positive directions of the) lines of the respective pleasure forces . . . let us employ an *arbitrary function* to denote the unknown *principle of compromise* between the parties . . . Then, by reasoning different from the preceding only in the point of view, it appears that the *total utility of the system is at a relative maximum at any point on the pure contract-curve*' (1881, pp. 24–5)

The important point about the contract curve for the analysis of exchange is of course that the locus of tangencies of indifference curves specifies the 'class of contracts to the variation of which the consent of *both* parties cannot be obtained' (1881, p. 28). Edgeworth's representation of the contract curve is shown in figure 3.1, where each axis measures the amount of the respective good exchanged (not consumed). As person A is assumed to hold all the

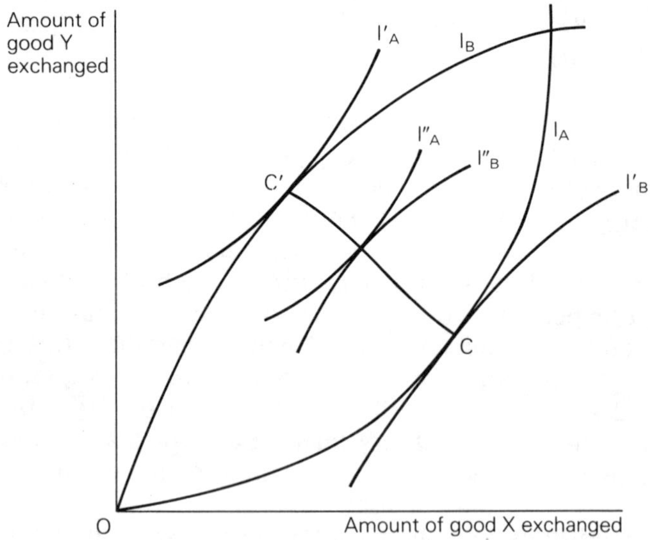

Figure 3.1 Exchange and the contract curve

initial stocks of good X, and none of good Y, the indifference curve which he can reach in isolation is shown as I_A, which passes through O. Similarly I_B is the indifference curve of person B which passes through O. Without trade they both *consume* at O, but they would obviously agree to any settlement in the area enclosed by I_A and I_B. The locus of efficient exchanges (such that movement would involve at least one party becoming worse off) is the contract curve CC′. Each point along CC′ represents a point of tangency, such as between I''_A and I''_B, or between I_A and I'_B which represents the best possible exchange for person B. Since exchange is the focus of attention, there is no need to specify the lengths of the axes in terms of the fixed supplies of the goods. The famous box diagram is obtained simply by specifying these lengths and drawing in the other two sides of the box.

In the diagram drawn by Edgeworth (1881, p. 28) he did not of course use a box construction. Furthermore the only indifference curves shown fully were those which each individual is able to reach in isolation, and which therefore specify the limits beyond which each is not prepared to move. Also part of the offer or reciprocal demand curves of each individual were drawn on the same diagram, although they were not defined until ten pages later (and were most fully discussed in an appendix). The term 'Edgeworth–Bowley Box' is often used, following Bowley's *Mathematical Groundwork of Economics* (1924) where it is introduced on the first page of the first chapter, but even Bowley does not actually draw a closed 'box'. The use of a box has of course no special analytical value, though it is perhaps a useful pedagogic addition. Many texts rotate Edgeworth's diagram though 90 degrees, and consider efficient *allocation*, rather than efficient *exchanges* with a specified initial endowment; thus a 'contract curve' would be drawn running the complete distance from the bottom left to the top right-hand corner.

After presenting the results for the two-person two-good case, Edgeworth (1881, p. 26) then examined the contract curve in the case where three individuals exchange three goods, stated that it is given by the 'eliminant', and then gave three lines of three sets of partial derivatives. In fact the contract curve in this context is defined by $|\partial U_i/\partial x_j| = 0$, where $\partial U_i/\partial x_j$ is the marginal utility of person i with respect to good j, but Edgeworth did not use the modern notation for determinants and did not set the Jacobian equal to zero. Furthermore the first line (containing the terms $\partial U_1/\partial x_j$; $j = 1, \ldots, 3$) appeared at the bottom of one page and the next two lines were placed at the top of the following page. It would not be surprising if what seems to be the first use of determinants in economics confused many of his readers.

The Problem of Indeterminacy

The concepts of indifference curves and the contract curve therefore help to specify a range of 'efficient exchanges' of goods between individuals. The essential feature of the analysis from Edgeworth's point of view is precisely that there is a *range*, rather than a unique point. This is clearly seen in figure 3.1 for two isolated traders where, 'the settlements are represented by an *indefinite number of points*' (1881, p. 29). At any particular settlement, the *rate* of exchange is expressed simply in terms of the amount of one good which is given up in order to obtain a specified amount of the other good: in terms of figure 3.1 it is the slope of the line drawn from the agreed contract to the origin O. Hence the existence of a range of efficient contracts along CC′ means that it can be said that the rate of exchange is 'indeterminate'. As Edgeworth stated: 'it is in the interests of both parties that there should be *some settlement*, one of the contracts represented by the contract curve between the limits. But *which* of these contracts is arbitrary in the absence of arbitration' (1881, p. 29). Any movement *along* the contact curve involves one person becoming better off at the expense of the other, and there is ample opportunity for disagreement. The rate of exchange achieved in practice will thus depend to a large extent on 'bargaining strength'. It was this result which led Edgeworth to make his often quoted remark that: 'An accessory evil of indeterminate contract is the tendency, greater than in a full market, towards dissimulation and objectionable arts of higgling.' (1881, p. 30).

Edgeworth argued that his analysis of indeterminacy in contract between two traders could be applied to a very wide variety of contexts. In particular, the tendency of large groups to form 'combinations', as in the case of trade unions and employers' associations, would serve to increase the extent of indeterminacy. Edgeworth's interest in wage bargaining has already been discussed earlier with reference to the Marshalls' discussion in their *Economics of Industry*, but he also examined at some length the example of contract about rent. The general applicability of his analysis of contract and indeterminacy was summarized by Edgeworth as follows: 'There emerges amidst the variety of construction and terminology πολλῶν ὀνομάτων μορφὴ μία [one shape with many names]' (1881, p. 31). This point is absolutely crucial to a full understanding of Edgeworth's work in economics, yet he used Greek at a vital stage in the argument! He expressed the same view rather more transparently in an appendix, where he said:

> What it has been sought to bring clearly into view is the essential identity (in the midst of diversity of *fields* and *articles*) of *contract*; a sort of unification likely to be distasteful to those excellent persons who are always dividing the One into the Many, but do not appear very ready to subsume the Many under the One. (1881, p. 146)

It is also of interest here that Plato's expression, 'the one in the many . . .' was later used by Marshall as the motto for his book on *Industry and Trade* (1919). Furthermore, in 1909 Marshall wrote to Edgeworth, saying, 'But yet I have a notion that I really have something to say . . . on the One in the Many and the Many in the One, ie the relations of details to fundamentals, a matter on which the experience of age is some atonement for its stupidity' (see Pigou, 1925b, p. 442).

Having shown the possibilities of indeterminacy, Edgeworth then went on to show how 'the escape from its evils' requires either competition or arbitration. The first of these is examined in the next chapter.

Further Reading

Edgeworth's rather late introduction to Jevons and Marshall certainly provides something of a mystery, but is not as uncommon as it might initially appear. Indeed, the mystery of Jevons's and Marshall's introduction to the work of Cournot is discussed by Hutchison (1955, pp. 7–8). Partly because Edgeworth, Sully and Jevons all lived in Hampstead, there is unfortunately very little correspondence among them. Part of a letter from Jevons to Sully is given in the volume edited by Jevons's wife (H. A. Jevons, 1886, p. 407), but Sully is mentioned only briefly (as a professor of Chemistry!) in the biography included in Black and Könekamp (1972, p. 50). Other members of the Savile included Bonamy Price, Fleeming Jenkin, Cliffe-Leslie, Leslie Stephen, T. H. Green and Henry Sidgwick. Clifford and Edgeworth were both members of the group of regular participants in Leslie Stephen's Sunday walks. It does seem surprising, given these connections, that Edgeworth did not know of the work of either Jevons or Marshall at an earlier date than 1879. But Keynes (1972, p. 148, n. 4) suggested that Edgeworth had no strong interest in economics before 1879, and he seems to have been very diffident.

There are several candidates for the authorship of the review of Jevons's *Theory of Political Economy* in the *Saturday Review* of 11 November 1871. Black (1981, p. 152) has suggested that it may have been written by George Wingman Hemming (1821–1905), a mathematician, lawyer and Fellow of St. John's College Cambridge who had a long association with the *Saturday Review*. He also published a book on income taxation (see Hemming, 1852). The present writer has suggested John Kells Ingram (1823–1907) as a strong possibility, in view of his mathematical ability and his negative statements about the use of mathematics in economics (Ingram, 1878; 1893). Young (1927, p. 217) attributes the review to Cairnes, but it seems that Young must have confused it with Cairnes's *Fortnightly Review* article of 1872. The question is discussed in detail in O'Brien *et al.* (1983), but because of the small sample size their statistical analysis is inconclusive.

The conventional analysis of Edgeworth's indifference curves and box diagram has been challenged by Tarascio (1972) and Jaffé (1974a), but these criticisms need not be taken seriously, as shown by Creedy (1980a). For further discussion of Marshall's use of 'the Many in the One and the One in the Many', see Whitaker (1975, Vol. 1, pp. 109–10; see also Vol. 2, p. 3).

The role of Bowley (1924) in spreading the use of the 'box diagram' was noted above, but also of importance is the fact that Marshall (1890) briefly discussed the contract curve, and presented a diagram, in his appendix on barter (see also chapter 5). The fact that Edgeworth's analysis of the role of the number of traders in competition (to be discussed in the following chapter) was ignored for so long is demonstrated by the strong statement of Schumpeter that, 'Marshall's *Principles* contains all that the reader needs to know about the barter theory as it had shaped before the century was out' (1954, p. 911, n. 7). A more complete and systematic discussion of exchange was that by Wicksell (1893), who nevertheless did not seem to have read *Mathematical Psychics*.

4

Competition and the Number of Traders

The central question which Edgeworth was trying to resolve in the second part of *Mathematical Psychics* was that of the conditions necessary to remove the indeterminacy which exists in the case of barter between two traders. The question naturally arises as to the extent to which this indeterminacy is the result of the absence of competition in the simple two-person market. Edgeworth thus quickly moved on to the introduction of further traders. His analysis of this problem, completed in just a few pages, is not easy to follow; indeed, it has taken many years for all the subtleties to be fully unravelled. The main purpose of this chapter is to examine, in section 4.1, Edgeworth's analysis of the implications of allowing for competition by introducing additional traders. It would not be helpful here to describe in detail Edgeworth's own method of presentation; the following provides a fairly non-technical explanation. Section 4.2 then considers Edgeworth's comments on Jevons's treatment of exchange (stimulated, as shown above, by the reviews of Jevons's book in the *Saturday Review*), and briefly notes some previous discussions of barter.

4.1 Additional Traders

The Recontracting Process

In Edgeworth's earlier problem of two traders exchanging two goods, the definition of a range of efficient exchanges (along the contract curve) is of course analytically separate from the question of whether or not two isolated traders would actually reach a settlement on the contract curve. However, these two aspects were not clearly separated by Edgeworth because right at the beginning of his analysis he introduced his stylized description of the process of barter: the famous 'recontracting' process. Edgeworth did not wish to assume at the outset that individuals have perfect knowledge. This contrasts with Jevons's treatment, since as part of his definition of a 'perfect' market Jevons explicitly assumed, in addition to his 'law of indifference', complete knowledge and product divisibility. Edgeworth continued to assume divisibility but instead of assuming initial perfect knowledge he supposed that, 'There is free communication throughout a *normal* competitive field. You might suppose the constituent individuals collected at a point, or connected by telephones – an ideal supposition, but sufficiently approximate to existence or tendency for the purposes of abstract science' (1881, p. 18). The knowledge of the other traders' dispositions and resources could then be obtained by the formation of tentative contracts which are not assumed to involve actual transfers, and can be broken when further information is obtained. Edgeworth introduced this in typical style:

> 'Is it peace or war?' asks the lover of 'Maud', of economic *competition*, and answers hastily: it is both, *pax* or *pact* between contractors during contract, *war*, when some of the contractors *without the consent of others recontract*. (1881, p. 17)

(The allusion here is to Alfred Tennyson's poem 'Maud; A Monodrama', part 1, verse VII). An important role of the recontracting process is thus to disseminate information among traders. It allows individuals who initially agree to a contract, which is not on the contract curve, to discover that an opportunity exists for making an improved contract according to which at least one person gains without another suffering. Edgeworth's stylized process does not direct attention to the role of information, or other well-known market 'imperfections', but provides a mechanism by which traders eventually reach a point on the contract curve.

The recontracting process is, however, not simply a convenient or artificial way of assuming that transaction costs are zero. Its real importance lies in the fact that it allows for Edgeworth's rich analysis of the role of the number of individuals in a market. With numerous individuals in a market the recontracting process makes it possible to analyse the use of collusion among some of the traders. Several individuals are thus allowed to form coalitions in order to improve bargaining strength and thereby improve each individual's gain from exchange. Recontracting then enables the coalitions to be broken up by outsiders who may attract members of a group away with more favourable terms of exchange.

The remarkable result then follows, as seen below, that the process of bargaining by forming and breaking coalitions will lead, if there is a sufficiently large number of individuals, to a unique settlement in which each person behaves *as if* he is responding *independently* to a specified rate of exchange. *The bargaining solution turns out to be equivalent to the price-taking equilibrium*. It may of course be suggested immediately that if there is a very large number of competitors, then no single individual can have any noticeable impact on the total amount of any good available. No individual would be able to depart from a common rate of exchange (or price ratio) in the rest of the market, and hence all traders would be price takers. But Edgeworth's analysis has the merit of providing the precise conditions under which this result would hold, and showing in a rigorous way how it would arise even allowing for collusion.

Two Additional Traders

The method of procedure was clearly stated by Edgeworth as follows:

> It is not necessary to resolve analytically the composite mechanism of a *competitive field*. It will suffice to proceed synthetically, observing in a simple typical case the effect of continually introducing into the field additional competitors. (1881, p. 34)

He began by introducing a second person A and a second person B, where the new traders are assumed to be exact replicas of the initial pair, having the same tastes and initial endowments. This simplification is very useful, because it enables the same diagram to be used as when only two traders are considered.

Two basic points can be stated immediately. The first point to stress is that in the final settlement which results from recontract both the As (and of course the Bs) must be treated equally. Since they are identical, no individual A can have any special advantage over his counterpart, and with convex indifference curves they would not settle for different allocations on the same indifference curve; a weighted average of two separate 'bundles' would get both individuals on to a higher indifference curve. The second basic point is that the settlement must be on the contract curve. These two results were clearly stated by Edgeworth as follows:

> It is evident that there cannot be equilibrium unless (1) all the field is collected at one point; (2) that point is on the *contract curve*. For (1) if possible let one couple be at one point, and another couple at another point. It will generally be the interest of the [A] of one couple and the [B] of the other to rush together, leaving their partners in the lurch. And (2) if the common point is not on the contract-curve, it will be the interest of all parties to descend to the contract-curve. (1881, p. 35)

The question at issue is whether the range of indeterminacy is reduced by the addition of these additional traders. Since the new A and B are identical to the old pair with respect to tastes and initial endowments, the same contract curve as before applies. But do all points on the contract curve qualify as *final* settlements?

Consider point C in figure 4.1(*a*), which is at the bottom right-hand extreme of the contract curve between the first pair of traders, who may be denoted A_1 and B_1. At this point B_1 clearly obtains all the gains from exchange and A_1 remains on the same indifference curve as can be reached in isolation; B_1 would require very strong bargaining power to attain such a position. Does the introduction of A_2 and B_2 affect this bargaining strength in any

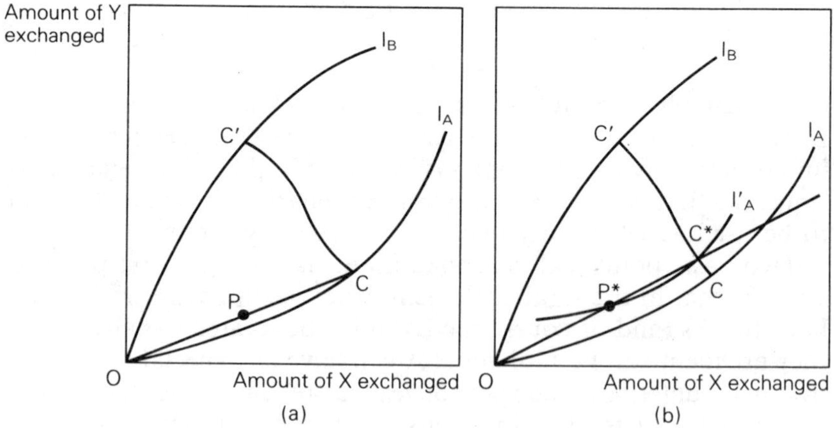

Figure 4.1 The introduction of additional traders

way? Suppose that B_1 attempts to form a contract with the two As, which still leaves B_1 at the extreme point C but leaves B_2 in isolation, or 'out in the cold'. Now it is evident that this would give an opportunity for A_1 to improve his position, since neither of the As would need to be at point C, along with B_1. The As have the amount of good Y received from A_1's trade with B_1 and they also have A_2's initial endowment of good X which has not been traded, in addition to A_1's remaining amount of good X. Any point along a straight line drawn between the origin O (A_2's initial position) and C (A_1's position after trade with B_1) represents an improvement for both of the As, since by assumption the indifference curve I_A is convex. For both individuals to be at the same point, however, they have to divide the amount of good Y obtained from B_1 into two equal portions; that is, they get half each. Hence they can reach the point P, in figure 4.1(*a*), which is half way along the ray from O to C. The common indifference curve of the As which passes through P is still 'higher' than I_A, so A_1 is better off than before while B_1 is just as well off as before, at C.

The arrangement can be shown algebraically as follows. Both As *begin* with initial endowments of $(a, 0)$, where the first term in parentheses is the amount of good X held and the second is the amount of good Y held. Similarly both Bs begin with $(0, b)$. If point C has coordinates (x, y), the contract places the two As at P, giving them $(a-x/2, y/2)$, B_1 at C with $(x, b-y)$, and B_2 in isolation with $(0, b)$. As before, x and y represent the amounts *exchanged*. This is obviously feasible, since the total amounts held after exchange of goods X and Y are $2a$ and $2b$ respectively. Person B_2 cannot prevent the coalition between the two As and B_1 taking place, but it is quite possible for him to make an offer to one of the As which would be mutually advantageous. One of the As could recontract with B_2, and B_1 would need to reconsider the situation. It would obviously not be possible to persuade the remaining A to trade at C, since the former could arrange yet another deal, with the other B, B_2, at highly advantageous terms to the latter, yet not as good as at point C. Furthermore, both As can be better off than at C by giving the best possible terms to only *one* of the Bs, so there is no longer any possibility of them both being forced to deal at C by the two Bs acting in collusion. This is because, without 'sympathy' for his counterpart, there is no incentive for the favoured B to bring the other out of isolation.

Hence B_1's strong bargaining power has been diluted by the competition from B_2. The situation was described by Edgeworth in the following terms:

> When this relation is satisfied the system of three might remain in the position reached; but for [B_2] who has been left out in the cold. He will now strike in, with the result that the system will be worked down to the contract-curve again; to a point at least as favourable for the [As] as [P]. Thus the [Bs] will have lost some of their original advantage by competition. (1881, p. 37)

Hence the best position that can be reached by the two Bs is a point, C* say, on the contract curve CC′ such that the As' utility at that point is the same ('at least as favourable') as at a point, P* say, positioned half way along a straight line from the origin to the point C*. (Remember that the As can reach only half way along the line from the origin to the point on the contract curve at which exchange with one of the Bs takes place.) The point along CC′ which is 'at least as favourable' as P* is shown in figure 4.1 (*b*) as C*. Here P* is half way along the new ray from O to C*, and the indifference curve, I'_A of the two As passes through P* *and* C*. Since no point between P* and C* can be attained by the As, C* must be the new limit to the contract curve. No individual B could get to a point between C* and C, because this would involve doing better than the other B, who could improve his own situation by offering an even better deal to one or both of the As.

The same kind of argument could also be applied to point C′, which can no longer be the best position reached by one of the As. In modern terminology it would thus be said that the *core* of the economy 'shrinks' as a result of the introduction of additional traders.

The Competitive Solution

If an additional pair of A and B is introduced the same kind of analysis can then be repeated. Can the former two Bs preserve their bargaining strength at point C*? Just as in the previous case, they could arrange a provisional contract with the three As which leaves them at C*, but leaves the third B out in the cold. The two previous As could improve their situation relative to C* since, with the additional A, they could reach a higher indifference curve than

I'_A by moving off the contract curve. In this situation if the two As were to share their traded amounts of good Y (obtained from the two Bs), and their remaining amounts of good X, with the third A (who has only his initial endowment of good X), all the As could reach a position two-thirds of the distance along the straight line between O and C*. Thus they can move to a point between P* and C* in figure 4.1 (*b*). They can reach *two-thirds* of the way along the line because the amount *y* of good Y, traded by each of the *two* Bs has to be divided among *three* As.

In the general case of a number *N* of each of the As and Bs, then the 'attainable' ratio of OP to OC is $(N-1)/N$, which has a limiting value of unity. From figure 4.1 (*b*) the point corresponding to P* would coincide with C*, and instead of an indifference curve I'_A cutting the ray from the origin and the contract curve at the new limit, the corresponding indifference curve would be *tangential* to the ray from the origin at the appropriate point on the contract curve. By definition there must be an indifference curve of the Bs which is also tangential to this indifference curve of the As at the new point on the contract curve; hence it must also be tangential to the same ray from the origin. The result of 'working in' from both extremes of the contract curve would then be a unique point on the contract curve, shown in figure 4.2, where the common

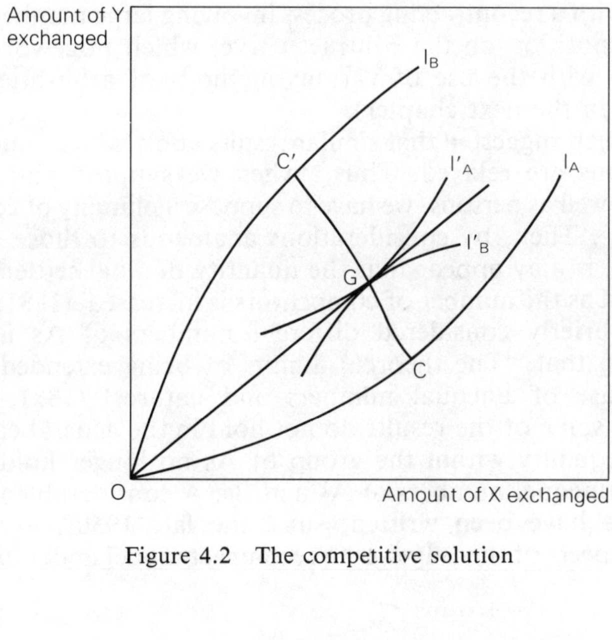

Figure 4.2 The competitive solution

indifference curve of the As is tangential to that of the Bs. After Edgeworth's much more terse discussion, he stated:

> If this reasoning does not seem satisfactory, it would be possible to give a more formal proof; bringing out the important result that the common tangent to both indifference curves at the point [G] is the vector from the origin. (1881, p. 38)

This last point made by Edgeworth is indeed very important. The significance of this result is that the vector from the origin is precisely the price vector which, if taken as given by traders, would achieve equilibrium in a market. The equilibrium solution where all individuals are independent price takers is therefore the same as that achieved by the recontracting process which allows for all kinds of collusive agreements. However, where all individuals are price takers they do not require any information about other individuals' tastes and stocks of goods; they need only know the equilibrium set of prices which they cannot influence in any way.

A further important implication of Edgeworth's result is that the competitive solution is necessarily on the contract curve. Much greater stress is usually placed on this result in modern expositions of economic theory, where it would be stated that the perfectly competitive equilibrium is 'Pareto efficient'. But Edgeworth placed more stress on the equivalence of the competitive price-taking solution with a recontracting process involving large numbers. This gave one position on the contract curve, which Edgeworth later compared with the use of various methods of arbitration (and discussed in the next chapter).

Edgeworth suggested that similar results apply when some of the assumptions are relaxed. Thus, 'when we suppose plurality of natures as well as persons, we have to suppose a plurality of contract-curves . . . Then, by considerations analogous to those already employed, it may appear that the quantity of final settlements is diminished as the number of competitors is increased' (1881, p. 40). He then briefly considered different numbers of As and Bs, concluding that, 'The theorem admits of being extended to the general case of unequal numbers and natures' (1881, p. 43). However, some of the results do not hold in the general case; for example equality within the group of As no longer holds when there are unequal numbers of As and Bs. A considerable number of articles have been written, since the late 1950s, examining various aspects of the Edgeworth recontract model under different assumptions. This is not, however, the place to consider these contributions, especially as several useful surveys already exist, and are listed at the end of this chapter.

One topical question to which Edgeworth applied his results, and to which he attached much importance, was that of the power of trade unions to increase wages. In this context the discussion of unions and wages in the Marshalls' *Economics of Industry*, mentioned above, is relevant. However, Edgeworth's statement was as always less prosaic:

> one thing from an abstract point of view visible amidst the jumble of catallactic molecules, the jostle of competitive crowds, is that those who form themselves into compact bodies by *combination* do not tend to lose, but *stand to gain* . . . in point of utility. (1881, p. 44)

Reciprocal Demand Curves

It has been mentioned that Edgeworth included in his diagram (1881, p. 28) the reciprocal demand curve, or offer curve, of each individual, although such curves were then called 'demand-and-supply curves'. Edgeworth mentioned them only briefly in the text (1881, p. 39), and again in his appendix on Jevons's formulae of exchange. The term 'offer curve' was not widely used until Bowley's *Groundwork* (1924), and in fact Edgeworth then objected to the expression (see also section 6.1, chapter 6). The lack of emphasis by Edgeworth is understandable, since in imperfect competition they are not relevant. In addition, they had been used very effectively by Marshall in his famous *The Pure Theory of Foreign Trade. The Pure Theory of Domestic Values* (1879). Edgeworth's contribution was to provide the basic 'analytics' of the offer curve in terms of indifference curves.

Transforming $U_A(x, y)$ to polar coordinates where ϱ measures the length from the origin along a ray inclined at an angle of θ to the x axis; then, 'tan θ expresses the *rate of exchange*. The demand curve [of A] is $[\partial U_A/\partial\varrho = 0]$. For this locus expresses the utmost amount of dealing to which the dealer will consent at any given rate of exchange . . . his utility is a maximum at that rate' (1881, p. 105). This may be seen as follows. If $U_A = U_A(x, y)$, then transforming to polar coordinates gives $x = \varrho \cos\theta$ and $y = \varrho \sin\theta$, and

$$\frac{\partial U_A}{\partial \varrho} = \frac{\partial U_A}{\partial x}\frac{\partial x}{\partial \varrho} + \frac{\partial U_A}{\partial y}\frac{\partial y}{\partial \varrho} = \frac{\partial U_A}{\partial x}\cos\theta + \frac{\partial U_A}{\partial y}\sin\theta$$

When $\partial U_A/\partial \varrho = 0$ then the ratio of marginal utilities $(-\partial U_A/\partial x)/(\partial U_A/\partial y)$, the slope of the appropriate indifference curve, is equal to $\sin\theta/\cos\theta = \tan\theta$, or the slope of the ray from the origin (remember that in Edgeworth's framework $\partial U_A/\partial x$ will be negative because x is the amount *exchanged*). Since the price ratio must equal the ratio of marginal utilities for constrained utility maximization, then the offer curve is, in Edgeworth's words, 'the locus of the point where lines from the origin *touch* curves of indifference' (1881, p. 113). This is shown in figure 4.3, which assumes, as before, that person A initially holds all the available stock of good X, and B holds the initial stock of good Y. This technique has subsequently been extended to cover the analysis of production using isoquants; and the treatment of offer curves in international trade analysis has been extended to include the production function, endowments of factors of production, and tastes, all in the same diagram, as in Meade (1952) (see also chapter 7).

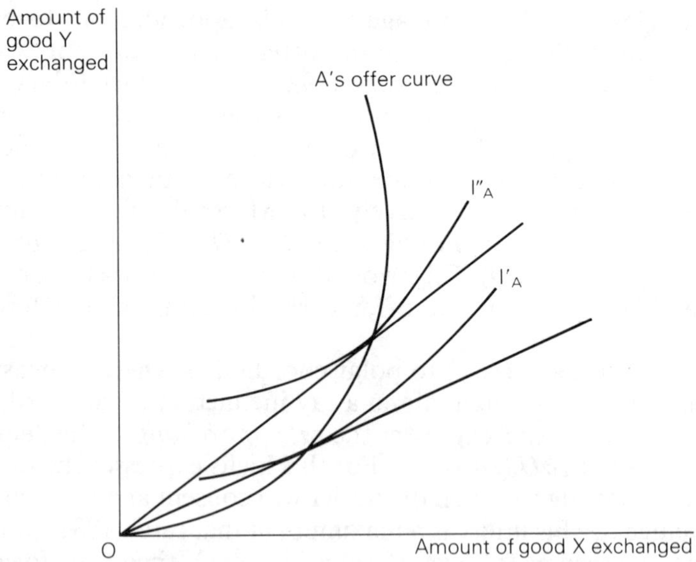

Figure 4.3 The reciprocal demand (offer) curve

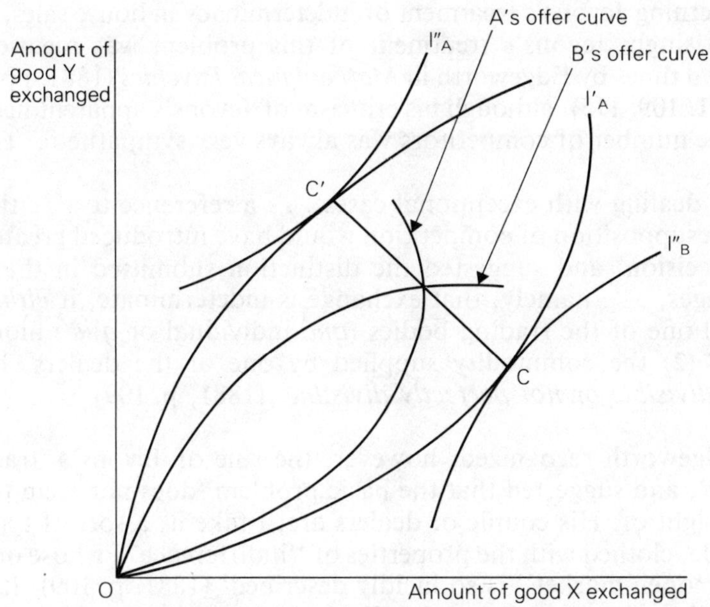

Figure 4.4 Equilibrium and offer curves

Figure 4.4 illustrates the important result that the price-taking equilibrium is at the intersection of the two offer curves, and this point must also be the competitive solution on the contract curve.

When, however, there is a lack of competition, giving rise to indeterminacy, there is nothing to ensure that individuals will trade on their offer curves. As Edgeworth argued: 'the conceptions of *demand and supply at a price* are no longer appropriate' (1881, p. 31), although his more general method could be applied both to price taking and imperfect competition. It is this general preference, in favour of the analysis of barter in non-competitive situations, to which Marshall objected in his *Academy* review of *Mathematical Psychics* (mentioned in chapter 3). Marshall's later support of his views, in the appendix on barter in his *Principles* (1890), will be discussed in chapter 6.

4.2 Further Discussion

Jevons and Indeterminacy

Section 4.1 examined the importance to Edgeworth of his contact with Jevons, and of the criticism of the *Saturday Review* reviewer concerning Jevons's treatment of indeterminacy in house sales. Not surprisingly Jevons's treatment of this problem was mentioned several times by Edgeworth in *Mathematical Psychics* (1881, pp. 19, 30, 31, 109, 115), although his criticism of Jevons's apparent neglect of the number of competitors was always very sympathetic. Thus:

> In dealing with exceptional cases . . . a reference to . . . the presupposition of competition would have introduced greater precision, and suggested the distinction submitted in these pages, . . . namely, that exchange is indeterminate, if *either* (1) one of the trading bodies (*quâ* individual or *quâ* union) or (2) the commodity supplied by one of the dealers, be *indivisible or not perfectly divisible*. (1881, p. 109)

Edgeworth recognized, however, the role of Jevons's 'trading body', and suggested that the basic problem 'does not seem to be lost sight of. His couple of dealers are, I take it, a sort of typical couple, clothed with the properties of "indifference", whose origin in a "open market" is so lucidly described' (1881, p. 109). It has sometimes been suggested that Edgeworth was much too generous to Jevons, although the balanced judgement of Black (1970) would seem the most sensible, and given the originality of Jevons's work it is not surprising that, 'There are indeed certain passages which admit of this interpretation, but equally there are others which do not' (1970, p. 267). An example of one which supports Edgeworth's interpretation is: 'The equation still more accurately represents the position of an individual consumer with regard to the aggregate trade of a large community, since he must buy at the current prices, which he cannot in an appreciable degree affect' (Jevons, 1957, p. 113).

It is perhaps not unreasonable to suggest that Jevons may have been led to introduce the concept of the trading body in response to the correspondence with Fleeming Jenkin (discussed in section 3.1, chapter 3). The correspondence, which took place in 1868, was all in terms of trade between two individuals 'Jones and Brown', so the trading body must have been a fairly late introduction to Jevons's argument. This suggestion is consistent with Edgeworth's comment quoted above, and of course Edgeworth did have the advantage of direct contact with Jevons.

Edgeworth placed his main emphasis on the need for a principle of arbitration in a 'world weary of strife' (1881, p. 51), since he anticipated a considerable increase in the extent of indeterminacy. The economical calculus therefore moves on to the utilitarian calculus, which formed the third part of *Mathematical Psychics* and will be examined in the following chapter. However, in view of the claim that Edgeworth's analysis of competition was highly original, it is first necessary to consider briefly a number of possible precursors.

Precursors of Edgeworth

The main emphasis in the journal literature is now mainly on Edgeworth's highly concentrated analysis of the role of numbers in competition, and on the 'tools of analysis' which he developed for that purpose (such as the contract curve). No serious training in economics would now be complete without a familiarity with these 'tools', with the result that the price-taking exchange equilibrium is on the contract curve, and that the barter settlement converges to the same position, as additional traders are introduced into the market.

Edgeworth's analysis of the role of numbers in competition was indeed a remarkable step in the development of economic theory. Many earlier economists had of course pointed out the characteristic indeterminacy which results from barter between two individuals. Furthermore, on an intuitive level the idea that a single individual in a very large market can have no noticeable impact on the total supply and demand was readily accepted. Indeed, an early statement can be found in Cantillon's discussion of markets, where he says:

> Suppose the Butchers on one side and the Buyers on the other. The price of Meat will be settled after some altercations, and a pound of Beef will be in value to a piece of silver pretty nearly as the whole Beef offered for sale in the Market is to all the silver brought here to buy Beef.
> The proportion is come at by bargaining. The Butcher keeps up his Price according to the number of Buyers he sees; the Buyers, on their side, offer less according as they think the Butcher will have less sale: the Price set by some is usually followed by others. Though this method of fixing Market prices has no exact or geometric foundation . . . it does not seem that it could be done in any more convenient way. (1755, p. 117)

Useful discussions of barter could be found in the works of Beccaria, Turgot, Isnard, Gossen, Courcelle-Seneuil, Thornton and Menger. Although Edgeworth was familiar with the works of some of these authors (in particular Beccaria, Gossen, Courcelle-Seneuil, and

Thornton) when writing *Mathematical Psychics*, the influence of Jevons and Marshall, discussed in section 3.1, is clearly the most important in tracing a direct line of filiation. Gossen and Beccaria are only mentioned (in 1881) in the context of the greatest happiness principle, and his ignorance of Menger's quite different discussion of barter has already been noted earlier.

More important is J. G. Courcelle-Seneuil, whom Edgeworth quoted approvingly (1881, p. 30) in the context of determinacy in large markets, referring to his example of indeterminate exchange between a hunter and a woodman. In his later brief discussion of 'barter' in Palgrave's *Dictionary of Political Economy* (Higgs, 1925, I, p. 122), Edgeworth praised Courcelle-Seneuil's discussion of additional traders. Courcelle-Seneuil in turn praised the work of Turgot, whose brilliant analysis was not, however, mentioned in *Mathematical Psychics*. Turgot's discussion, partly reproduced in Meek (1973, pp. 77–100), is without doubt of a very high quality in many respects, but its analysis of the role of numbers is 'highly suggestive' rather than conclusive. Furthermore, Cournot's (1838) analysis, involving the introduction of additional firms into a monopoly until a competitive market is reached, was actually criticized by Edgeworth for not allowing for indeterminacy when numbers are small. He wrote:

> This gradual 'extinction' of the influence of monopoly is well traced by Cournot in a discussion masterly, but limited by a particular condition, which may be called *uniformity of price, not (it is submitted) abstractedly necessary in cases of imperfect competition*. (1881, p. 47)

Although the subject of indeterminacy had often been discussed before Edgeworth, along with the general idea that competition would reduce the range of indeterminacy, there is therefore really nothing that comes close to Edgeworth in terms both of rigour and clarity of purpose. Stigler was surely correct to state that, in terms of his analytical contribution, 'Edgeworth was the first to attempt a systematic and rigorous definition of perfect competition' (1965, p. 241). Even viewed by the narrower standard of modern economics, which prefers to eschew any mention of utilitarianism, Edgeworth's achievements in this respect were considerable.

The way in which Edgeworth used his results, concerning the 'Economical Calculus', to provide a new justification of utilitarianism as a principal of distributive justice, has, however, suffered considerable neglect. This is examined in the following chapter.

Further Reading

Edgeworth's discussion of wage bargaining was praised by Webb and Webb (1919, p. 647). The conventional interpretation of recontracting has been challenged by Walker (1973), but for criticism of Walker's argument see Creedy (1980a).

The earliest rigorous analysis of Edgeworth's analysis of the role of numbers in competition, in terms of recently developed theories of co-operative games, was in the important paper by Shubik (1959). For more extensive treatments and bibliographies, see the texts by Bacharach (1976) and Hildebrand and Kirman (1976). Edgeworth's analysis is placed in context in two surveys, concentrating respectively on 'micro-foundations of macroeconomics' and game theory, by Weintraub (1977) and Schotter and Schowodiauer (1980). The list of papers concerned with 'Edgeworth market games' and 'limit theorems' is far too long to give here. The term 'core' was not in fact used by Edgeworth, except that he referred to the 'controlless core' of human selfishness (1881, p. 52).

Further discussion of Turgot is in Groenewegen (1970). Beccaria and Isnard are mentioned briefly by Schumpeter (1954, pp. 306–7). Rather extravagant claims for Aristotle and Gossen are made by Jaffé (1974b), whose discussion is distorted by his idiosyncratic view of Edgeworth's analysis (see also Jaffé, 1974a). Edgeworth's comments on Böhm-Bawerk's later discussion of horse trading will be mentioned in chapter 6.

The correspondence between Jenkin and Jevons, concerning indeterminacy, has already been discussed in chapter 3 and in section 4.2. It is perhaps surprising that Edgeworth did not mention Jenkin's important 1868 paper on trade unions (Jenkin, 1931). Jenkin (1931, pp. 82–7) discussed auctions, mentioned Thornton's case of Dutch and English auctions, and even used the example of horse trading. Also of significance is his statement that, 'in simple transactions between man and man for one object . . . neither demand nor supply curves can be drawn' (1931, p. 86).

5

The Utilitarian Calculus

It has been seen in chapters 3 and 4 that Edgeworth's main objective, in his section of *Mathematical Psychics* on the 'Economical Calculus', was to show the general conditions under which barter would result in an indeterminate rate of exchange. He showed how the range of indeterminacy is reduced when the number of traders on 'each side of the market' increases, and how a unique determinate exchange rate results from competition among a very large number of traders. Furthermore, this rate of exchange was shown to be precisely the same as the equilibrium price ratio; that is, the price ratio which ensures that there are no excess supplies or demands when all individuals take prices as fixed beyond their control. Edgeworth contrasted the price-taking model of Jevons and Walras with his own analysis in which the uniform equilibrium price arises from the recontracting process. In the Walrasian model the 'auctioneer' obtains all the required information without cost, and has the authority to set the equilibrium price (and does so without payment in a disinterested manner). However, in Edgeworth's analysis competitors acquire information through the free process of recontracting. In each case all transaction costs are assumed to be zero.

For Edgeworth the existence of indeterminacy in many contexts had even wider implications; it led him to a deeper 'justification' of utilitarianism as a principle of distributive justice. It is this somewhat neglected aspect of Edgeworth's analysis which is examined in section 5.1. Having arrived at this new link between 'impure' (egoistic) and 'pure' utilitarianism, Edgeworth had only to reorientate his earlier analysis of optimal distribution. The results of his paper in *Mind* of 1879, containing a more general treatment of the subject than his book of 1877, then acquired a new significance. Edgeworth simply reprinted that paper with only minor changes, as the third part of *Mathematical Psychics*. This is discussed briefly in section 5.2.

5.1 Contractarian Utilitarianism

The Need for Arbitration

The crucial development of Edgeworth's utilitarianism arose from the recognition that, once indeterminacy is shown to exist, there is a need for arbitration. Indeed, Jevons had stated clearly that with indeterminacy:

> The dispositions and force of character of the parties . . . will influence the decision. These are motives more or less extraneous to a theory of economics, and yet they appear necessary considerations in this problem. It may be that indeterminate bargains of this kind are best arranged by an arbitrator or third party. (1957, pp. 124–5)

Edgeworth's statement of the same point was as usual rather less prosaic:

> The whole creation groans and yearns, desiderating a principle of arbitration, and end of strifes. (1881, p. 51)

He often stressed the problems arising from indeterminacy, giving rise to 'the Art of Bargaining – higgling dodges and designing obstinacy, and other incalculable and often disreputable accidents' (1881, p. 46). The really crucial step taken by Edgeworth involved the justification of utilitarianism as a 'principle of arbitration'. This step involved two basic arguments. First, in considering alternative principles of justice which might perhaps serve the purpose, Edgeworth argued that they must at least place individuals on the contract curve. For example, dividing all goods equally among the parties would not be satisfactory since there is no presumption that the arrangement would be on the contract curve. Therefore:

> . . . the self interests of the two parties will *concur* to bulge away from the assumed position; and, bursting the cobwebs of doctrinaire justice, to descend with irresistible force to some point on the contract curve. (1881, pp. 54–5)

The same point applies to the principle of 'splitting the difference', although Edgeworth was rather less critical, regarding it as the outcome of a 'rudimentary "implicit" justice' (1881, p. 55).

This first requirement of a principle of justice is, however, met by the utilitarian principle that the sum of individual utilities should be maximized. The utilitarian objective is, in the case of two individuals, simply to maximize $U_A + U_B$, the first-order conditions for which are $\partial U_A/\partial x + \partial U_B/\partial x = 0$ and $\partial U_A/\partial y + \partial U_B/\partial y = 0$. Multiply the first conditions by $\partial U_B/\partial y$ and the second by $\partial U_B/\partial x$, and subtract the resulting equations to obtain an expression which is the same as the standard equation of the contract curve shown in equation (3.4) of chapter 3. The importance of this result to Edgeworth cannot be exaggerated. As he said:

> It is a circumstance of momentous interest that one of the in general indefinitely numerous *settlements* between contractors is the utilitarian arrangement . . . the contract tending to the greatest possible total utility of the contractors. (1881, p. 53)

He had of course also demonstrated that the competitive, price-taking, equilibrium is on the contract curve. Thus competition might be viewed as a kind of impersonal arbitrator, simultaneously setting the rate of exchange and the distribution of the gains from exchange. In cases of indeterminacy it might be argued that an arbitrator should attempt to determine the equilibrium position which would correspond to a competitive market formed by many replicas of the two parties. But Edgeworth explicitly argued against this, saying that, '. . . it is tenable that there is an adjustment of contracts more beneficent than that which the mechanical play of competition tends to establish' (1925, ii, p. 284).

Edgeworth's Justification of Utilitarianism

Edgeworth recognized that although it could be shown that the utilitarian solution is on the contract curve, this result was not *sufficient* to justify the use of utilitarianism as a principle of arbitration. The contract curve defines a *range* of positions. It is only a *necessary* condition of a principle of arbitration that it should place the parties somewhere on the contract curve. If they are not on the contract curve, then of course at least one party can gain without the other losing. Edgeworth's justification for utilitarianism as a principle of justice, comparing points *along* the contract curve, was as follows:

> Now these positions lie in a *reverse order of desirability* for each party; and it may seem to each that as he cannot have his own way, in the absence of any definite principle of selection, he has about as good a chance of one of the arrangements as another . . . both parties may agree to commute their chance of any of the arrangements for . . . the utilitarian arrangement. (1881, p. 55)

The important point to stress about this statement is that Edgeworth clearly viewed distributive justice in terms of *choice under uncertainty*. He argued that the contractors, faced with uncertainty about their prospects, would choose to accept an arrangement along utilitarian lines. A crucial component of this argument, also clearly stated by Edgeworth in this quotation, is the use of equal a priori probabilities; this is the suggestion that 'each party . . . has about as good a chance of one of the arrangements as another'. The use of equal a priori probabilities recurs many times in his work (as pointed out in chapter 1) and, for example, was also used by him in his later (Bayesian) analysis of statistical inference contained in his third and last monograph, *Metretike* (1887). Thus, 'there is made an assumption, not statistically verified, concerning the equi-distribution of a priori probabilities' (1887, p. 56).

Edgeworth was, as has already been stressed, extremely conscious about the wide gulf between theory and practice, but the importance to him of this new justification of utilitarianism cannot be exaggerated. Indeed the whole of *Mathematical Psychics* seems to be imbued with a feeling of excitement generated by his discovery of a justification based on a 'social contract'. This provided the crucial link between 'impure' and 'pure' utilitarianism in a more satisfactory way than his earlier appeal to evolutionary forces. Furthermore, with perhaps an allusion to Butler (see chapter 2), he suggested that, 'It is far from the spirit of the philosophy of pleasure to depreciate the importance of religion; but in the present inquiry, and dealing with the lower elements of human nature, we should have to seek a . . . more earthly passage, from the principle of self-interest to the principle . . . of utilitarianism' (1881, pp. 52–3).

Edgeworth clearly believed that he had provided an answer to an age old question that had defeated so many earlier utilitarians. Thus he stated that:

> by what mechanism the force of self-love can be applied so as to support the structure of utilitarian politics, neither

Helvetius, nor Bentham, nor any deductive egoist has made clear. (1881, p. 128)

This feature of *Mathematical Psychics* was, however, ignored for many years. It was even overlooked when, following the development of the von Neumann–Morgenstern approach to choice under uncertainty, major 're-statements' of utilitarianism were made by Harsanyi (1953, 1955) and Vickrey (1960). The maximization of expected utility, with each individual taking the a priori view that any outcome is *equally likely*, was shown to lead to the use of a social welfare function which maximizes the sum of individual utilities. This approach is now usually described as 'contractarian neo-utilitarianism'.

Edgeworth's statement was, however, later acknowledged by Rawls, who said that a contractarian approach, 'is sometimes suggested by Bentham and Edgeworth, although it is not developed by them in any systematic way' (1971, p. 29). Rawls described this approach as a 'deeper and more roundabout justification of utilitarianism' (1971, p. 29), although of course he rejected it in favour of his own 'maxi-min' approach (see especially Rawls, 1971, p. 170). Nevertheless, the contractarian approach can also be shown to lead to the maxi-min rule if it is assumed that each individual has extreme risk aversion (see Atkinson and Stiglitz, 1980, pp. 339, 420; Phelps, 1973, pp. 418–23).

It may be true that Edgeworth did not write down a mathematical proof of his argument for utilitarianism, as did Vickrey and Harsanyi, but his contractarian view was much more important to Edgeworth than Rawls suggested. Furthermore, the same justification of utilitarianism was offered by Edgeworth in his later analysis of income taxation. He rejected the quid pro quo view of taxation, on the argument that public expenditure and taxation decisions do not result from competitive exchange processes. Some principle of justice is required in the framework of a social contract between taxpayers and government. In deciding on the appropriate tax burden, Edgeworth suggested that:

> each party may reflect that, in the long run of various cases . . . of all the principles of distribution which would afford him now a greater, now a smaller proportion of the sum-total utility obtainable . . . the principle that the collective utility should be on each occasion a maximum is most likely to afford the greatest utility in the long run to him individually. (1925, p. 102)

Edgeworth's analysis of taxation will be examined in more detail in chapter 7, but it can be seen here that the explicit treatment of the question of taxation in contractarian terms involves the direct link between the analyses of the appropriate tax burden and of the optimal utilitarian distribution. The use of the criterion of minimum total sacrifice (requiring equal marginal sacrifice) was then of course only a small step to take. This approach of Edgeworth marked an important stage in the process of bringing the analysis of taxation within the general framework of 'welfare economics', involving standard welfare criteria rather than a special set of 'tax maxims'.

Thus Edgeworth's justification of utilitarianism along contractarian lines was clearly and explicitly articulated, and was more important to Edgeworth than is generally recognized. After his analysis of the need of 'a world weary of strife' for a principle of arbitration, this approach to the use of utilitarianism became the critical link between the 'economical' and the 'utilitarian' calculus.

It must also be stressed that Edgeworth referred to his contractarian justification on a number of later occasions not mentioned by Rawls (1971), and right up to the age of 80 when he prepared his *Papers Relating to Political Economy* (1925) for publication. Edgeworth returned to the question of indeterminacy and arbitration in his important survey of the theory of distribution (1904, rep. 1925, i). He again argued in favour of the utilitarian principle and referred back to relevant passages of *Mathematical Psychics* (see 1925, i, p. 57). In editing his *Papers*, Edgeworth added a cross-reference to volume ii (p. 101) where the same argument was made in the reprint of the taxation paper. The same point is referred to again (1925, ii, p. 322).

In the present context it is also worth considering Edgeworth's later comment on Gossen, who was only mentioned briefly in *Mathematical Psychics* (1881, p. 94). In one of his many contributions to Palgrave's *Dictionary*, Edgeworth wrote:

> Gossen is guilty of a fallacy to which mathematical economists are peculiarly liable: what may be called the 'illicit process' from the principle of utility in economics to utilitarianism in the philosophy of conduct. The logical error is aggravated in the case of Gossen by a certain pedantry and want of humour. (Higgs, 1925, ii, p. 233)

Edgeworth's critical remark here arises from his objection to what he sees as Gossen's 'social harmony' approach, in contrast with his own explicit recognition of the 'strife' and 'higgling' which give rise to the need for a principle of arbitration. Gossen had confused the market *equilibrium* position with that which maximizes the sum of individual utilities. It is interesting that Walras (in his second edition of the *Elements*) criticized Gossen on similar grounds, arguing that the utilitarian solution would require compulsion and would therefore not be acceptable (see Walras, 1874, p. 205 and the last subsection of the present chapter). But this is precisely where Edgeworth's argument is important, because he showed that individuals (assuming equal a priori probabilities of outcomes) would *voluntarily agree* to a social contract accepting utilitarianism as a principle of distributive justice. Edgeworth believed that he had indeed provided a legitimate process leading from the principle of utility in economics (the economical calculus) to utilitarianism in the philosophy of conduct (the utilitarian calculus).

5.2 Arbitration and Distribution

Interpersonal Comparisons

Having shown the need for a principle of arbitration in indeterminate contract, Edgeworth then stated his result that the utilitarian arrangement is one of the positions along the contract curve, and presented his argument that 'both parties may agree to commute their chance of any of the arrangements for . . . the utilitarian arrangement' (1881, p. 55). It must be recognized that until Edgeworth reached the analysis of the need for a principle of justice in 'the universal sigh for articles of peace' (1881, p. 51), no concept of *cardinal* utility was required, and no interpersonal comparisons were made. Edgeworth was actually quite explicit on this point:

> For moral calculus a further dimension is required; to compare the happiness of one person with the happiness of another, and generally the happiness of groups of different members and different average happiness. (1881, p. 7)

His attitude was that 'such comparisons can no longer be shirked' (1881, p. 7), since they are so often required in the consideration of practical problems. Questions of distribution were never far from

Edgeworth's mind, and indeed this applies to many of his contemporaries who had approached economics via moral philosophy. To be entirely agnostic, or nihilistic (as many later economists were to become) about distributional outcomes would have been unthinkable to Edgeworth. A similar view was taken by Marshall, who observed that:

> It is useless to say that various gains and losses are incommensurable, and cannot be weighed against one another. For they must be, and in fact they are, weighed against one another before any deliberate decision is or can be reached on any issue. (Pigou, 1925a, p. 302)

Edgeworth did not minimize the problems involved in making such comparisons, though he often stressed the importance of 'sympathy' as the means by which individuals make inferences about the well-being of others. His considerable caution with regard to the practical use of these theoretical results (mentioned in chapter 1) should also be stressed. In this context he stated, for example, that they provide, 'a star affording a general direction, not a finger-post to specify a by-path' (1881, p. 56). The subject of ordinal and cardinal utility will again be raised in section 6.1 of the following chapter.

The Utilitarian Solution

The analysis of this third part of *Mathematical Psychics* consisted, as already stated, of a reprint of most of Edgeworth's earlier article in *Mind* (1879). This in turn extended the results of the *New and Old Methods of Ethics*, and handled the problems with much more assurance. His main emphasis, as before, was to argue that utilitarianism does not necessarily imply equality.

However, before reprinting those results, Edgeworth pointed out in a footnote (1881, p. 53, n. 1) that the argument, demonstrating that the utilitarian solution is somewhere on the contract curve, is not affected by the existence of 'sympathy'. If the contractors are not entirely egoistic, but actuated 'by a sympathy for each other's interests' then the range of indeterminacy will also be reduced, although the rest of the contract curve remains as before. This may be seen by setting the first person's objective at $U_A + \lambda U_B$ and that of the second person at $U_B + \mu U_A$. It can be shown that in this case the contract curve is given by

$$\frac{\partial U_A/\partial x+\lambda\partial U_B/\partial x}{\partial U_A/\partial y+\lambda\partial U_B/\partial y}=\frac{\partial U_B/\partial x+\mu\partial U_A/\partial x}{\partial U_B/\partial y+\mu\partial U_A/\partial y} \tag{5.1}$$

which can be rearranged to give the same result as in the standard case. Thus 'sympathy' simply reduces the range of indeterminacy, along the same contract curve as in the case of egoism. Thus Edgeworth's main argument covers the whole range from impure (egoistic) to pure (universalistic) hedonism. However, in discussing the utilitarian solution as a principle of arbitration in indeterminate contract, Edgeworth did not clearly indicate in 1881 that the utilitarian solution of maximum total utility could specify a position which makes one of the parties worse off than in the no-trade situation. This was nevertheless later made explicit when, after proposing arbitration along utilitarian lines, he added, '. . . subject to the condition that neither should lose by the contract' (1925, ii, p. 102). This possibility of course depends largely on the initial endowments of the individuals.

When Edgeworth reproduced from *Mind* (1879) his analysis of the optimal utilitarian distribution he made no attempt to improve the clarity of the exposition. It would have been very difficult, if not impossible, for most contemporary economists to follow the details of the argument, especially as he made extensive use of the calculus of variations. He examined not only the distribution of the 'means of pleasure' but also that of the 'work done'. It is perhaps useful here to set up the basic problem in discrete form, and using a simple Lagrangian approach rather than the much more versatile calculus of variations. The problem described below corresponds to that in *Mathematical Psychics* (1881, pp. 66–8).

Edgeworth discussed the utilitarian optimal distribution in terms of each individual's capacity both for work and for pleasure, represented by the variable x. He was not very explicit about the nature of this 'capacity' for work and pleasure, but acknowledged that it would be more 'elegant' to regard x as a 'variable in terms of which both capacities may be expressed'. Let $F_i\ (x_i,\ y_i)$ represent the 'pleasure' of the ith individual ($i=1, \ldots, N$) with 'capacity' x_i and 'means' y_i. Further, let $f_i\ (x_i,\ p_i)$ be the 'work done' by person i, which is a function of 'capacity' and 'pain', p_i. The utilitarian objective is to maximize the sum of pleasure over pain; that is

$$\sum_{i=1}^{N}\ (F_i-p_i)$$

subject to the constraint that $\Sigma y_i = \Sigma f_i$, or that total 'work done' equals total 'means'. The Lagrangian is then given by

$$L = \Sigma(F_i - p_i) - c\Sigma\ (y_i - f_i) \tag{5.2}$$

and the first-order conditions for a maximum are

$$\begin{aligned} \frac{\partial L}{\partial y_i} &= \frac{\partial F_i}{\partial y_i} - c = 0, \qquad i = 1, \ldots, N \\ \frac{\partial L}{\partial p_i} &= c\frac{\partial f_i}{\partial p_i} - 1 = 0, \qquad i = 1, \ldots, N \end{aligned} \tag{5.3}$$

and

$$\frac{\partial L}{\partial c} = \Sigma y_i - \Sigma f_i = 0$$

The solution therefore requires

$$\frac{\partial F_i}{\partial y_i} = 1/\frac{\partial f_i}{\partial p_i} = c \qquad i = 1, \ldots, N \tag{5.4}$$

Equation 5.4 corresponds to the solution to Edgeworth's more general problem (1881, p. 68). As the appropriate matrix of second-order derivatives takes a very simple form it is easy to see that the conditions $\partial^2 F_i/\partial y_i^2 < 0$, $\partial^2 f_i/\partial p_i^2 < 0$ for all i are sufficient to guarantee a maximum, and to satisfy the condition that y_i and p_i can be solved as functions of x_i (that is, the Jacobian, which is the determinant of the matrix of second derivatives, is non-zero). Even using simple functional forms for F_i and f_i it is nevertheless very difficult to obtain the explicit solutions for p_i and y_i. Edgeworth was, however, mainly concerned to interpret the conditions shown in equation (5.4). The general implication is that those more capable of pleasure should have more 'means' and more pleasure, while those most capable of working should do more work, and suffer more pain. He was careful to point out that this assumes that 'the means of pleasure and the pain of work are *independent* variables' (1881, p. 68). It may be added that when reviewing *Mathematical Psychics* Jevons took the opportunity to quote Edgeworth's results on the distribution of 'pains' and 'rewards' back to him. Jevons stated:

'Would it be too much to ask of Mr. Edgeworth that when he prepares his next work he will endeavour to save the labour of his readers, even at the expense of his own labour. In fact, may we not apply to the author his own theorem . . .?' (1881, p. 583).

The analysis was extended to consider the appropriate (utilitarian) growth of population, allowing differential growth among families with different abilities. Here the influence of Galton is clearly evident. This type of exercise is now unlikely to find many sympathetic readers, especially when suggesting that because 'higher' (more cultured) pleasures are more 'pleasurable', there is, 'a reason deeper than Economics may afford for the larger pay, though more often more agreeable work, of the aristocracy of skill and talent' (1881, p. 78). It is here where Edgeworth refers to the 'supposed' superior capacity of man for happiness, and quotes:

Woman is the lesser man, and her passions unto mine
Are as moonlight unto sunlight and as water unto wine. (1881, p. 78)

(This is another of Edgeworth's unattributed and inaccurate quotations drawn from memory; it is in fact from Tennyson's 'Locksley Hall'.)

After 1881 Edgeworth did not return to his mathematical analysis of the utilitarian calculus; and it is indeed doubtful if any further 'mileage' could be made from it. The economical calculus, on the other hand, provided the basis of much of his later work in economics, which will be examined in subsequent chapters. It is useful first to examine some of the statements of Edgeworth's contemporaries on utility maximization. It becomes clear, not surprisingly, that his contribution of 1881 made little immediate impact within a wider group of economists.

Later Views on Welfare Maximization

It has been seen that Edgeworth, having defined the contract curve as a locus of efficient exchanges, showed that the competitive equilibrium (of price-taking individuals and of a large number of traders engaged in barter) is one of the points along the contract curve. He went on to argue that this point does not necessarily coincide with the arrangement that maximizes total utility (considered as a sum of individual utilities), although the latter is also on the contract curve. The utilitarian arrangement is necessarily on the contract curve because it implies equal ratios of marginal utilities (ignoring, as Edgeworth did for most of his discussion, the possibility that one of the parties may be made worse off relative to the no-trade position, depending on the distribution of initial endowments).

The modern textbook treatments of welfare economics now usually concentrate on the first statement above, where it is said that the competitive equilibrium is one of an infinite number of 'Pareto efficient' allocations (defined to include the complete set of allocations, rather than only efficient *exchanges*). Interpersonal comparisons of welfare are now the responsibility of a social welfare function, which specifies the appropriate point on a utility possibility curve for the achievement of maximum social welfare. These issues have now been clarified and are included in any serious training in economics. It is, however, of some interest to see that the general clarification of these points in the literature did not follow in quite so straightforward a manner; indeed, there was much confusion and Edgeworth's contribution was neglected even by those who admired his work. The main figures are Walras, Launhardt, Pareto and Wicksell, and as in many economic debates it is not a straightforward matter to distinguish the problems of logic from those of logomarchy.

The debate was often framed in terms of the question of whether or not government intervention could improve upon the competitive equilibrium, but it was often confused by the lack of a clear distinction among types of gain. It was not always clear whether the discussion concerned the relative maximum utility of each individual constrained by facing fixed prices, the total gains from trade, or the total utility resulting from the final allocation of goods. At the end of section 5.1 it was mentioned that Walras (in the second edition of the *Elements*) criticized Gossen essentially for confusing the competitive equilibrium with the utilitarian maximum. However, the difficulty and often the lack of clarity of Walras's writing seems to have led Launhardt (1885) to accuse Walras of wrongly suggesting that the competitive equilibrium maximizes total utility after exchange. Wicksell also accused Walras of giving 'in several passages' . . . 'a wrong or at least misleading formulation' (1893, p. 19), and went on to say that, 'it would indeed be the remarkable attribute of free exchange to call forth the greatest possible economic gain or total satisfaction' (1893, p. 13). However, Wicksell later defended Walras against such an accusation, and it does indeed seem that Walras had only the first type of constrained, or relative, utility maximization in mind. This view is indeed supported by the (above mentioned) note on Gossen where Walras said that the position of maximum total utility, 'is not the relative maximum utility of free competition' (1874, p. 205). Interpretation of Walras is of course complicated by the fact that, as Robbins suggested, 'no one would contend that the exposition of the [*Elements*] . . . is a model of expository clarity' (Wicksell, 1901, Introduction p. xi).

Wicksell was, however, less generous to Launhardt. Wicksell (1893, p. 67) gives a numerical example where the *gains* from exchange, for two price-taking individuals in equilibrium, are equal. He then says in a footnote that Launhardt gave a similar example, recognizing that he was dealing with a special case. But Wicksell later accused Launhardt of arguing that competition actually maximizes total utility (see 1893, p. 76, n. 2; 1901, p. 81, n. 1). Wicksell's inconsistency here is difficult to explain, especially as Launhardt's purpose was precisely to show that maximum total utility is only attained in competition under very special circumstances (see Hutchison, 1953, pp. 187–8). This point was recognized quite clearly by Pantaleoni (1889, p. 161, n. 1) who cited Launhardt and Marshall as providing caution, 'against the mistake of inferring . . . that [the competitive equilibrium] coincides necessarily with that which realises the maximum of general happiness'.

It is therefore rather unfortunate that Samuelson (1947, p. 205), citing only Wicksell's *Lectures*, actually 'credits' Launhardt with being, 'the only economist who attempted to give rigorous proof' of the theorem that competition maximizes total utility. Samuelson went on to say that, 'we can learn more from his unambiguous failure than from many pages of fuzzy literary effusion'. More interesting, however, is the fact that neither Wicksell, Pantaleoni, nor Samuelson mention Edgeworth's analysis in *Mathematical Psychics*. Of course Wicksell and Pantaleoni may have experienced difficulty in obtaining a copy of the privately printed book. When Wicksell discussed indeterminacy (1901, p. 51) he referred to Edgeworth indirectly, giving the source as Marshall's *Principles*, and when he accused Pareto and Marshall of paying insufficient attention to indeterminacy (1958, p. 143) he referred to Edgeworth's Italian review of Marshall's *Principles* in the *Giornale degli Economisti* of 1891. (This review will be discussed in more detail in the next chapter.)

Wicksell was more consistent in his criticisms of Pareto's *Cours*. He argued that, 'throughout the book [Pareto] reasons as if the gain from exchange were at an absolute maximum under free competition, and that, moreover, it is so for each trading subject (which actually involves a mathematical absurdity)' (1958, p. 143). Wicksell justified his argument using the same mathematical analysis as in the *Lectures* (1901, p. 81), and also criticized Pareto for not having read Marshall's *Principles* sufficiently carefully (especially the latter's analysis of decreasing cost industries). In reviewing the *Manuel*, Wicksell later criticized Pareto's now famous criterion, according to which welfare is maximized, and argued that Pareto had not clearly recognized that it is satisfied at an infinite number of points, one of which is actually a welfare minimum rather than a maximum (1958, p. 168). Wicksell's criticism was of course quite valid, and it is worth noting that what is now called the Pareto criterion of efficiency was initially proposed by Pareto as his definition of what he thought of as a unique maximum social welfare; to say that 'the contract curve is a locus of Pareto efficient allocations' therefore distorts historical perspective somewhat. Pareto's errors arose partly, Wicksell argued, because of his failure to give sufficient emphasis to indeterminacy in exchange. Pareto's lack of attention to this issue is perhaps surprising in view of the fact that he turned to the serious study of economics as a result of contact with Panteleoni. In the *Manuel* Pareto did not mention Wicksell (1893), nor did he refer explicitly to Edgeworth's *Mathematical Psychics*. More attention has been given in the literature to Pareto's work, largely as a result of that of Hicks and Allen in the 1930s, but it is worth quoting the judgement of his great friend and mentor Pantaleoni, that 'Pareto . . . elaborated a system of general economic equilibrium . . . with materials only partially his own, . . . he would not have been what he has been without . . . [Edgeworth and Fisher]' (1923, p. 584). In view of the general discussion of this and other issues it is perhaps not surprising that Edgeworth felt there was a significant role for mathematics in 'correcting fallacies', but it seems unfortunate that his own 'currency' was not circulated more widely.

Further Reading

Although Rawls (1971, p. 172) rejected the approach to his 'maximin' criterion via choice under extreme risk aversion, he initially seemed to give it some support (see Rawls, 1967, p. 61, n. 2). Mirrlees (1982) has more recently considered utilitarianism in terms of preferences with regard to allocations to 'alternative selves'. For criticism of the approach see Pattanaik (1968). On this aspect of Edgeworth's approach see also Creedy (1984b).

For further discussion of the effects of sympathy see Collard (1975, 1978, pp. 18–29). Edgeworth argued that, with differing utility functions, utilitarianism does not imply equality. Lerner (1947) later argued that if the functions are unknown there is a high probability that total utility is maximized by equality. 'Probabilistic egalitarianism' was also discussed by Sen (1973, pp. 83–5) who, in his view, 'rescued' the argument from its utilitarian framework.

For some notes by Marshall on maximizing total utility, with reference to Edgeworth's approach, see Whitaker (1975, pp. 317–19). On the application of his argument in favour of the utilitarian arbitration, the following comment by Robertson (on Edgeworth's two lectures on 'Political Economy and War', 1916) is of interest: '. . . here is Professor Edgeworth nothing daunted, with all the modesty of true learning and all the polyglot graces of his unique style, gently thrusting as it were before the noses of statesmen and diplomatists the principle of the maximization of aggregate utility as a possible solvent of their differences' (1931, p. 219).

Pantaleoni (1889, p. 161), when commenting on competition and utility maximization, referred to Alfred and Mary Paley Marshall's discussion of differences in the marginal utility of income of different individuals, but Wicksell (when criticizing Pareto) referred to Marshall's discussion of decreasing cost industries. When discussing indeterminacy, Pantaleoni (1889, p. 145) referred to house sales and mentioned Dutch and English auctions (with reference to A. and M. P. Marshall), but did not refer to Edgeworth's analysis, although he elsewhere referred generally to *Mathematical Psychics*. Menger's discussion of indeterminacy was discussed by Wicksell (1958, pp. 198–200), but as noted earlier it was not known to Edgeworth in 1881. Confusion over the idea that perfect competition produces an 'ideal' situation of course also extended to J. B. Clark's synthesis of marginal productivity theory: Edgeworth's brief criticism of Clark in this respect is noted in the following chapter.

6

Further Work on Exchange and Distribution

After the publication of *Mathematical Psychics*, Edgeworth concentrated increasingly on mathematical statistics, in particular on the problem of statistical inference. In addition to the long stream of papers in the *Journal of the Royal Statistical Society*, his third and last monograph was published in 1887. This was *Metretike: or the Method of Measuring Probability and Utility*, and of course the subject represents a natural progression from his earlier two monographs. However, the book received little attention, and Keynes (1972, p. 261) remarked that, 'It is a disappointing volume and not much worth reading (a judgement with which I know that Edgeworth himself concurred)'. During this period Edgeworth also produced his important work on index numbers, a subject to which he regularly returned in later years.

Following his appointment to the Drummond Chair at the age of 46, and his editorship of the *Economic Journal*, Edgeworth again made important contributions to economics. As discussed in chapter 1, his work often took the form of extended commentaries on the writings of others. This chapter examines the main contributions in the area of exchange and distribution, many of which stem directly from work contained in *Mathematical Psychics*. Section 6.1 considers developments in the area of demand analysis. The analysis of monopoly and oligopoly, largely arising from the earlier work on indeterminacy, is examined in section 6.2. Edgeworth (1881, p. 47) had criticized Cournot for assuming uniformity of prices, and had gone, 'beyond Cournot, not without trembling'. Rather less diffidence was displayed in his later work, however. Section 6.3 then considers further work on distribution, including his treatment of production.

6.1 Demand Theory

It has been stressed in earlier chapters that Edgeworth's concepts of indifference curves and the contract curve were introduced as an integral part of his analysis of exchange and the distribution of the gains from exchange. Although he showed how offer curves for an individual facing fixed prices can be derived from a set of indifference curves, this was given very little emphasis as attention was concentrated on barter in markets without price taking. Only where there is a large number of competitors are the price-taking and recontracting solutions identical. Edgeworth briefly pointed out that the competitive equilibrium was also the point of intersection of the two offer curves in the case where the market consists of replicas of the initial pair of traders.

The techniques were not used, as in so many modern text books, to examine the implications for partial equilibrium demand curves. Despite Edgeworth's considerable interest in statistical inference, he made no attempt to estimate demand curves and indeed argued that, 'Jevons' hope of obtaining demand curves by statistical observation . . . may appear chimerical' (Higgs, 1925, i, p. 473). This view may be contrasted with the much more optimistic statement of Marshall that, 'as time goes on, the statistics of consumption will be so organised as to afford demand schedules sufficiently trustworthy' (Pigou, 1953, p. 25). This section is thus mainly concerned with Edgeworth's reactions to, and discussions arising from, the later work of other authors.

Marshall and Indeterminacy

In the *Principles of Economics* (1890, Appendix F) Marshall included a brief discussion of Edgeworth's analysis of barter, and produced a figure showing the contract curve. During the following year, in the course of a review written in Italian, Edgeworth criticized Marshall for not having dealt sufficiently with the problem of indeterminacy. Marshall's letter in reply was deeply felt:

> What I want to say is that I do not think you at all appreciate the deadly and enduring injury that A does to B, if he reads rapidly a piece of hard argument on which B has spent an immense deal of work; and then believing that argument to be wrong, writes an article full of the most polite phrases, in

which a caricature of that argument is held up to the most refined, but deadly scorn. I fancy you think that the polite phrases diminish the mischief . . . Their effect . . . is that of a white flag under which the ship approaches close to another and rams or torpedoes it . . . There! I feel so much better: I am like a person who has held his mouth full of air under water for a minute. (Marshall, 1890, pp. 796–8)

Marshall also recruited Arthur Berry to publish a response to Edgeworth's article. Berry had provided help with the mathematical appendix to the *Principles*, and knew Italian. His own contribution to marginal productivity theory was also noteworthy (see Baumol and Goldfeld, 1968, pp. 313–15). The basic problem was that Marshall had believed that his assumption of an additive utility function, combined with the assumption that the marginal utility of one good is constant for both individuals, guaranteed a determinate price, if the 'good' having constant marginal utility was of course money. Indeed, this case was mentioned by Edgeworth in his 1891 review (and later in 1925, ii, p. 317, n. 1). If $U_A = U_1\,(a-x) + \alpha y$ and $U_B = U_2\,(x) + \beta y$, then the contract curve can be shown to be given by $U_1'\,(a-x)/U_2'\,(x) = \alpha/\beta$. Hence x is constant and the contract curve is a straight line parallel to the y axis. The problem still arises that the total amount spent on the good x is indeterminate, but Edgeworth was reluctant to push his point, writing, 'as one who has already burnt his fingers and fears the fire of controversy' (Marshall, 1890, p. 798).

There was, however, a later, though much milder, disagreement between Marshall and Edgeworth over the so-called Giffen good. Most students are now introduced to the concept of the Giffen good using indifference curve analysis and the decomposition of the effect of a price change into income and substitution effects (see Hicks, 1939, p. 35). But Edgeworth did not use such an analysis and was not concerned with the theoretical *possibility* of an upward sloping demand curve, but with its *probability*. In reviewing a book by Rea, Edgeworth argued that:

> Even the milder statement that the elasticity of demand for wheat *may* be positive, though I know it is countenanced by high authority, appears to me so contrary to *a priori* probability as to require very strong evidence. (1909, p. 104)

The 'authority' was of course Marshall (1890, p. 132), who replied directly to Edgeworth that, 'I don't want to argue . . . But . . . the matter has not been taken quite at random' (Pigou, 1925a, p. 438). However, Marshall had no convincing empirical evidence, and the 'paradox' has, like many other issues, taken on a life of its own in textbooks; references can now be found, without any statistical evidence, to commodities such as rice and the Irish potato.

Additivity and Complementarity

Edgeworth's introduction of the general (rather than additive) utility function has already been discussed in chapters 2 and 3. Schumpeter calls the generalization 'an obvious improvement' (1952, p. 127), but apart from the fact that so many innovations only seem obvious with the advantage of hindsight, the implications are far from straightforward. Edgeworth himself later said that, 'the whole rigid system bursts up in a universal *debâcle*, as we relax the assumption that the [marginal] utility of one commodity is independent of that of the others' (1925, iii, p. 38). The concepts of indifference curves and the contract curve do not of course depend on the generalization of the utility function, and the widespread acceptance of the general form was extremely slow (see Stigler, 1965, p. 105; Blaug, 1968, p. 330). Many leading economists continued to use the additive form well into the twentieth century; even Fisher (1927) later used independence in his attempt to measure marginal utility, while Pigou (1910) needed to make the assumption for his method of measuring price elasticities from household budgets. The additive form is still used in most theoretical work on intertemporal allocation problems and in many empirical demand studies for reasons of tractability.

Those who were reluctant to use the general form could also appeal to Marshall's statement that, 'Prof. Edgeworth's plan of representing U and V as general functions of x and y has great attractions to the mathematician; but it seems less adapted to express the every-day facts of economic life than that of regarding, as Jevons did, the marginal utilities of apples as functions of x simply' (1890, p. 844). Nevertheless, much of Marshall's analysis in the text of the *Principles* explicitly allows for significant interdependencies.

An immediate implication of the generalized utility function is that it allows for complementarity. Edgeworth did not explicitly consider this in 1881, for the obvious reason that he concentrated on contract and indeterminacy, although after stating his assumption that $\partial^2 U_A/\partial x \partial y < 0$, he noted in parentheses that, 'attention is solicited to the interpretation of the third condition' (1881, p. 34). The first formal definition of complementarity is attributed to Auspitz and Lieben, and it was used by Edgeworth in his paper on the pure theory of monopoly (1925), discussed later in this chapter, and also by Pareto. This defines commodities i and j to be complements (substitutes) if $\partial^2 U/\partial q_i \partial q_j > 0$ (<0); with $U = U(q_1, \ldots, q_n)$, and the qs are the amounts consumed. This type of complementarity is now often referred to, using the initials of the four people mentioned above, as ALEP complementarity. When discussing Auspitz and Lieben's contribution, Samuelson condescendingly says that it was, 'not bad work for bankers' (1974, p. 1279). However, among non-English European economists their work was very highly regarded. When later discussing their treatment, using offer curves, of what is essentially the optimum tariff argument, Edgeworth praised their, 'beautiful and original reasoning' (1925, ii, p. 295).

The first major criticism came from Johnson (1913), who pointed out that the criterion was not invariant with respect to monotonic transformations of the utility function. Johnson's treatment was extended by Allen (1934) and by Hicks and Allen (1934), so that the modern definition involves *compensated* price changes. Thus q_i is defined as a *net* substitute (complement) for q_j *if* $\delta q_i/\delta p_j > 0$ (<0), where the use of δ indicates that the price change is compensated, that is retaining constant utility. If uncompensated changes are considered, the goods would now usually be called *gross* substitutes, but there is no symmetry between gross substitutes and complements as only the matrix of (compensated) substitution elasticities is assumed to be symmetric. If the matrices of price and substitution elasticities are respectively $\{e_{ij}\}$ and $\{s_{ij}\}$, and the vectors of budget shares and income elasticities are respectively $\{w_j\}$ and $\{e_j\}$; then Slutsky's equation is simply $e_{ij} = s_{ij} - w_i e_j$. Edgeworth later accepted Johnson's point but argued that the earlier definition would still be useful in some contexts (1925, ii, p. 465), and was 'more intrinsic'.

Edgeworth's comment on Johnson's (1913) paper does raise a minor question, however. It has often been noted that Johnson did not refer to the important and highly relevant work of Fisher and Pareto (discussed in the next subsection). But this work was well known to Edgeworth, who was of course editor of the *Economic Journal* where Johnson's paper appeared. Furthermore (as seen in chapter 4) Edgeworth thought that the term 'offer curve' was first used by Bowley (1924), although it appears clearly in Johnson (1913).

It thus seems that Edgeworth did not pay very much attention to Johnson's paper when he first saw it.

Ordinal Utility

It is now well known that Fisher (1892) independently 'discovered' the indifference curve analysis, showed the conditions under which a cardinal concept of total utility may be avoided, and in so doing considered the integrability problem for more than two goods. Edgeworth had a very high opinion of Fisher, as seen from his statement that, 'we may at least predict to Dr. Fisher the degree of immortality which belongs to one who has deepened the foundations of the pure theory of economics' (1925, iii, p. 41). The following extract, from a letter by Fisher's wife to her mother-in-law after Fisher had lectured at Oxford (following Edgeworth's invitation), gives some idea both of Edgeworth's behaviour and of his respect for Fisher:

> On the way out I saw Professor Edgeworth and so introduced myself. He was very nice (but rather surprised I think at my speaking to him), but then he went on to say how 'Dr. Irving Fisher is *soaring*'. They always call each other by their full name here. (see I. N. Fisher, 1956)

The term 'soaring', borrowed from Sidgwick, was high praise indeed. Pareto's later analysis, involving the movement, via integration, from the slopes of indifference curves to utility functions, was also reviewed favourably by Edgeworth (1925, iii).

Following this and later work which showed that demand and expenditure functions are invariant with respect to monotonic transformations of the utility function, so that only an ordinal concept of utility is required and the indifference curve analysis can be reworked only in terms of marginal rates of substitution, Edgeworth's utilitarianism is often regarded as an unnecessary late Victorian addition. For example Schumpeter, with an almost violent abhorrence of utilitarianism, stated that, 'Edgeworth professed utilitarianism in season and out of season. Yet analysis shows that these professions may be struck out from his economic propositions without being missed' (1954, p. 780; see also p. 831). This issue will again be raised in chapter 8.

6.2 Monopoly and Oligopoly

Competition, in one form or another, had for long been the standard assumption in economic literature. It has been seen that Edgeworth's analysis in *Mathematical Psychics* led him to predict a 'considerable extent of indeterminateness'.

He was quite clear about the implications for economic theory. The result would be 'to impair . . . the reverence paid to *competition*; in whose results – as if worked out by a play of physical forces, impersonal, impartial – economists have complacently acquiesced' (1881, p. 50).

His later statement was even stronger, suggesting that in a regime of oligopoly the role of abstract economics would be much reduced and, 'there would survive only the empirical school, flourishing in a chaos congenial to their mentality' (1925, i, p. 138). A similar view was also expressed in the well-known statement of Hicks (1939, p. 84) that abandoning the competitive assumption would involve the 'wreckage of the greater part of economic theory'.

Until the late 1920s and 1930s there had indeed been very little work on the analysis of monopoly or oligopoly, and the situation was clearly summarized by Marshall when he wrote that, 'Cournot led the way, and among those who have made chief advances in it Professors Edgeworth and Pigou are prominent. Readers are referred to their masterly work . . .' (1919, p. 399). Edgeworth's contribution actually first appeared in Italian in 1897, and was not available in English until he provided a translation for inclusion in the *Papers* (1925). Initially the paper produced more response for its analysis of the taxation of monopolists, which will be examined in the following chapter. The present section concentrates on his discussion of indeterminacy which of course arose directly from the earlier work of 1881 and revolves around his criticism of Cournot.

Criticism of Cournot

Edgeworth begins with Cournot's example of the 'source minerale' in which there are 'two monopolists' (that is, *duopolists*), each owning a spring of mineral water. Cournot had arrived at a determinate solution for price and output but Edgeworth showed how, 'when two or more monopolists are dealing with competitive groups, economic equilibrium is indeterminate' (1925, i, p. 116). The daily output from each spring was assumed to be limited to identical fixed amounts; delivery costs were assumed to be zero; and all consumers had the same demand curve. It was implicitly assumed that each consumer purchases only one unit of output, so that sales are increased by attracting more customers. The demand x is then given by $N(1-p)$, where N is the number of customers and p is the unit price.

If each duopolist deals separately with N customers, giving a total of $2N$ customers shared, then the price which achieves maximum revenue is $p = 1/2$. Thus only half of the maximum possible output is sold. But each duopolist is selling an identical type of good, so that there is an incentive for one of the duopolists to lower his price, and deprive his rival of part of his initial custom. The rival will of course follow suit and, 'by successive steps . . . the price may be lowered to ¼, which is just sufficient to take off the whole supply of one monopolist offered to half the market' (1925, i, p. 119). This is Cournot's solution, but Edgeworth then argued that although no one has an incentive to lower the price further, one of the duopolists may *increase* his price back to ½; that is, back to his revenue maximizing price. This is because his rival, 'has already done his worst by putting the whole of his supply on the market. The best that the rival can do . . . is to follow the example set him and raise his price to ½' (1925, i, p. 120). There is of course no reason why the process should end at this stage, since from the earlier argument there is an incentive for one of the duopolists to reduce his price again. Thus instead of there being a determinate stable solution, Edgeworth stated that 'there will be an indeterminate tract through which the index of value will oscillate' (1925, i, p. 118).

This rather extreme statement of the result implies continually fluctuating prices, and has not surprisingly been criticized as unrealistic. However, it seems most appropriate to interpret the indeterminacy here in the same way as in the theory of exchange; it shows that other conditions are required in addition to the profit maximizing assumption. The recontracting process discussed in chapter 4 may also appear to imply a type of dynamic process, but it is of course an entirely static analysis. In a sense, recontracting may be seen as a *deus ex machina* to get individuals onto the contract curve, to facilitate the analysis of barter involving the formation of coalitions, and to allow concentration on final settlements independently of the 'paths' taken. The framework of analysis of the duopolists (Edgeworth's 'two monopolists') really contains no dynamic element at all. Furthermore Edgeworth quickly qualified his statement concerning oscillation by suggesting that:

> at every stage . . . it is competent to each monopolist to deliberate whether it will pay him better to lower his price against his rival as already described, or rather to raise it to a higher . . . for that remainder of customers of which he cannot be deprived by his rival. . . . Long before the lowest point has been reached, that alternative will have become more advantageous than the course first described. (1925, i, p. 120)

In a later discussion Edgeworth was much more explicit about the lack of a true dynamic element in the theory, when he stated that, 'of course I do not suppose such a prolonged series of steps . . . to occur in the concrete. But I think it is a legitimate fiction in order to bring out the contrast with competition, which tends to a definite . . . equilibrium' (1925, ii, p. 101, n. 1).

Reaction Curves and Isoprofit Lines

It is characteristic of Edgeworth that he went on to say: 'the matter may be put in a clearer light'. However, in the next sentence he defined what is now called the *reaction curve* and *isoprofit lines* (in that order) for variations in prices. In fact, it was not really until Bowley's *Groundwork* (1924) that these matters began to be put in a more transparent manner. Edgeworth's accompanying diagram (1925, i, p. 120) is also difficult to follow since it represents the extreme case of perfect substitutes where prices must ultimately be identical.

Consider, however, figure 6.1 which shows, for a general case, the two sets of isoprofit and reaction curves for two duopolists A and B (Edgeworth's 'monopolists'). These curves are drawn here as

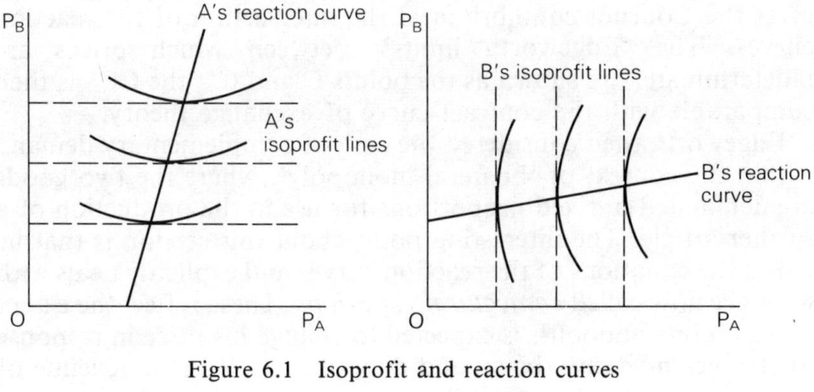

Figure 6.1 Isoprofit and reaction curves

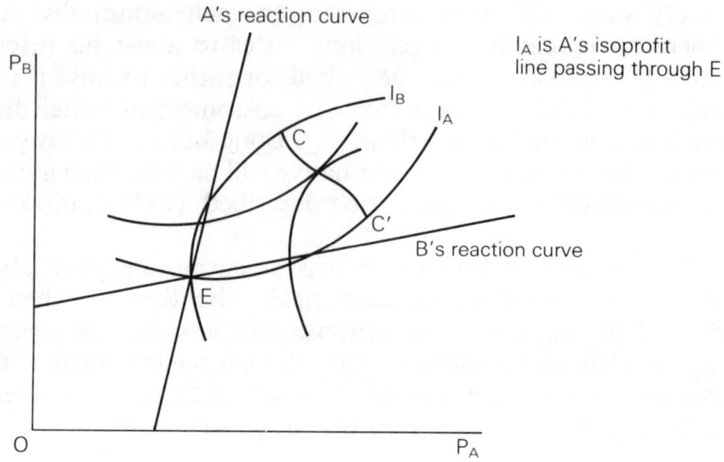

Figure 6.2 Edgeworth limits

straight lines for convenience only. Where, 'ξ and η are the coordinates representing the prices of the articles', the reaction curve was defined by Edgeworth as:

> The locus of maximum profit for the monopolist owning the commodity x, of which the price is ξ – the *watershed*, so to speak, of the utility surface for that monopolist (or more exactly the locus of that price of x which for any assigned price of η affords maximum profit to the owner of x). (1925, i, p. 121)

The isoprofit lines are obviously comparable with indifference curves. Placing the two parts of figure 6.1 together in figure 6.2 gives the Cournot equilibrium at the intersection of the reaction curves. The 'Edgeworth limits', between which prices are indeterminate, are shown as the points C and C′; the CC′ is then comparable with the contract curve of exchange theory.

Edgeworth then considered the case of complementary demand within the context of 'bilateral monopoly', where the two goods are demanded in fixed proportions for use in the production of a further article. The interesting point about this section is that he writes the equations of the reaction curves and explicitly deals with what are now called *conjectural variations*. These reflect the extent to which one duopolist is expected to change his price in response to changes made by the second duopolist. If V is the revenue of the second monopolist and P_i the prices ('abstracting cost of production'), Edgeworth criticized Cournot for assuming that the duopolist will set $\partial V/\partial P_2 = 0$, whereas 'he will go on varying the price P_2 until . . . $\partial V/\partial P_2 + (\partial V/\partial P_1)\, \partial P_1/\partial P_2 = 0$' (1925, i, p. 123). It is the term $\partial P_1/\partial P_2$ which denotes the conjectural variation.

In discussing this problem Edgeworth then introduced a further important concept which is fundamental to the modern theory of games. This is the 'saddle point', which he called the 'Hog's Back'. Edgeworth clearly indicated its importance for stability. However, he admittedly used, 'a somewhat fanciful illustration' of two Arctic explorers moving at right angles to each other on the ice (1925, i, p. 124). Thus again is not surprising, but unfortunate, that a long time had to elapse before Edgeworth's contribution was fully appreciated.

6.3 Production and Distribution

Given the general importance to Edgeworth of the theory of exchange in economics, it should not be surprising that his views on production and distribution were dominated by his approach to exchange. Thus the first sentence of his survey of the theory of distribution is a direct statement of his approach: 'Distribution is the species of exchange by which produce is divided between the parties who have contributed to its production' (1925, i, p. 13).

This survey resulted from lectures delivered at Harvard, and first published not, as usual, in the *Economic Journal* but in the *Quarterly Journal of Economics* in 1904. However, it does not, unfortunately, represent the kind of synthesis which Edgeworth attempted in his earlier treatments of taxation and international values, which are discussed in the following chapter. It is perhaps too much a commentary on contemporary theories, and contains little that is really constructive. Historians of economic thought have tended to concentrate on Edgeworth's discussion of the alternative definitions of the nature of the entrepreneur, in particular the 'no-profit entrepreneur' of Walras. This is the main subject of the following subsection. The related issue of Wicksteed and linear homogeneous production functions is also briefly discussed.

The No-profit Entrepreneur

In his *Elements*, Walras (1874, p. 225) had introduced the concept of the entrepreneur who neither gains nor loses. This result applied only to the competitive static equilibrium, where there are no incentives for 'entrepreneurs' to enter any industry. This does not of course mean that there are no profits, in the accounting sense, since the returns to (homogeneous units of inputs of) organization and management services are subsumed in the costs of the firm. Most modern students of economics are quickly introduced to the corresponding concepts of 'normal' and 'supernormal' profits, and know that in the perfectly competitive equilibrium all firms are of equal size and earn only normal profits.

Edgeworth's criticisms of the concept of the no-profit entrepreneur (contained in his review of the second edition of the *Elements*, repeated in his 1904 survey, and reproduced in his *Papers*) have usually been summarily dismissed by leading historians of thought. For example Hutchison (1953, p. 205) simply commented that the concept, 'evoked some not very well directed mockery from Edgeworth'. Schumpeter, for whom Walras is a favourite, was as usual more dogmatic, stating that, 'The almost violent aversion towards Walras' concept, first by Edgeworth . . . is therefore wholly unjustified and rests on nothing but a complete failure to understand Walras' (1954, p. 1049, n. 59). Neither critic really examined Edgeworth's argument, however, and it can easily be seen that he is innocent of their charge of misunderstanding Walras.

Edgeworth in fact clearly recognized that with Walras's assumptions there was nothing illogical about the argument. He stated quite clearly that the theory means that nothing remains, 'after the entrepreneur has paid a normal salary to himself' (1925, i, p. 26; see also p. 30). Furthermore, 'if [the general expenses] are taken into account, the argument becomes *a fortiori*. For why should not a substantial remuneration for the entrepreneur be included in the general expenses of the business' (1925, ii, p. 469). Edgeworth's difference with Walras was, as he clearly acknowledged, 'only verbal'. Thus:

> While we accept the ideas, we are not bound to adhere to the words of a master . . . It is violently contrary to usage; it lends itself to a dangerous equivogue; and it has led distinguished economists to paradoxical conclusions. (1925, i, p. 25)

Indeed, the modern terminology – involving normal and supernormal profits rather than a concept of zero profits – can be seen to meet Edgeworth's objections.

It is, however, worth adding that Edgeworth also expressed some doubts about treating the entrepreneur as being 'like that of any other labour' (1925, i, p. 26), though he saw clearly the analytical convenience in describing competitive equilibrium conditions. He stated that it was 'the exact mathematical analogy between the marginal product of the entrepreneur and that of an operative in a large establishment which I dispute' (1925, ii, p. 380), and he was not happy with the idea that 'entrepreneurship' was homogeneous and divisible. Later critics of the neoclassical 'theory of the firm' would no doubt be more sympathetic towards Edgeworth's criticisms of Walras.

It is appropriate at this point to refer to Edgeworth's criticism of Wicksteed (1894), where the input of the entrepreneur was treated just as any other factor, and where the assumption of a linear homogeneous production function ensured that all the 'product' was distributed as factor payments in accordance with the marginal productivity theory. Edgeworth's famous remark is worth repeating:

> This is certainly a remarkable discovery: for the relation between product and factors is to be considered to hold good irrespectively of the play of the market . . . There is a magnificence in this generalisation which recalls the youth of philosophy. Justice is a perfect cube, said the ancient sage; and rational conduct is a homogeneous function, adds the modern *savant*. (1925, i, p. 31)

What Edgeworth really objected to was Wicksteed's ambitious statement that the theory would hold in *any* type of market, including Robinson Crusoe's island, an American religious commune, an Indian village ruled by custom and in modern industries (see Wicksteed, 1894, p. 42). Given Edgeworth's emphasis, in *Mathematical Psychics* and elsewhere, on the problems of indeterminacy and the conditions required for competition to produce a determinate set of price ratios, it is not really surprising that he objected so strongly to Wicksteed's statement. However, Wicksteed was elsewhere more careful to point out that his result required competitive equilibrium conditions. Edgeworth was not of course alone in attacking Wicksteed, as further major criticisms were directed by Pareto (see for example Baumol and Goldfeld, 1968, pp. 321–5). It is pertinent to recall that at this time the marginal productivity theory had not been fully developed, and there was no abstract theory of the firm along modern lines.

The question of indeterminacy and the use of a principle of justice in distribution was then discussed explicitly by Edgeworth in his 1904 survey; this mainly involved a terse repetition of points he had made earlier. He took the opportunity to argue, against Clark, that competition and payment according to the marginal productivity theory does not necessarily give rise to an 'ideal' distribution (1925, i, p. 52), and alluded to his 'contractarian utilitarianism'; the basic issues have been discussed in chapter 5. He stated that arbitration would require a comparison of gains and losses, for which the 'cultivation of sympathy' (that is; mutual understanding) is necessary. In discussing indeterminacy he also examined Böhn-Bawerk's famous example of horse trading, in which limits to the price range were specified, but argued that, 'it is riding a one-horse illustration to death to put the accident of an exceptional sort of auction as representative of the actual transactions by which the great mass of national income is distributed' (1925, i, p. 39). However, he accepted that his criticism, 'involved an issue about which legitimate differences of opinion may exist'.

Further Reading

For further details concerning so-called Giffen goods, see Schultz (1938, pp. 51–4), and Stigler (1965). On Marshall's position see also Gramm (1970) and Dooley (1983). The case of the Irish potato is thoroughly dealt with in Dwyer and Lindsay (1984). On interrelations of demand, the work of Schultz (1933) is also important (see also Schultz, 1938, pp. 22–4). A general discussion is contained in Samuelson (1974), who says (p. 1279) that Edgeworth assumed complementarity; but in view of the problem arising from Edgeworth's specification of the utility functions in terms of the amounts exchanged rather than consumed, his intention is not entirely clear. It is difficult to accept Stigler's interpretation of Edgeworth's acknowledgement of Auspitz and Lieben's work, that he, 'was so punctilious in acknowledging predecessors that his tone suggests independence of discovery' (1965, p. 192). Strangely Stigler (1965, p. 134) found it, 'difficult to see the purpose' in Johnson's or in the Hicks–Allen definition of complementarity, on the dubious grounds that, 'they cannot be applied introspectively'. However, Chipman (1977) has shown that the 'ALEP' definition still has empirical implications. On the empirical implications of assuming additivity see Deaton (1974). On the derivation of the utility function by integration from marginal rates of substitution, Edgeworth was clearly impressed by Fisher's contribution and discussion of the 'integrability' problems arising. He commented, 'Soaring . . . beyond the furthest heights of his predecessors; . . . he attains . . . a conclusion which seems to us of unexpected value' (1925, iii, p. 40). On Pareto's later analysis of the same problem, it is interesting to learn from Pantaleoni that Pareto's first publication was on the theory of elasticity in solid bodies and, 'researches concerning the integration of the differential equations determining their equilibrium' (1923, p. 584). On these aspects see also Creedy (1979).

The work of Pigou on monopoly and oligopoly which Marshall had in mind (in 1919) was presumably Pigou (1908). For further discussion of Edgeworth's treatment of duopoly see Nichol (1935) and Farrell (1970). Edgeworth also used the analogy of a game of chess, which has been used in almost every analysis of oligopoly. A valuable analysis of the problems is by Zeuthen (1930), who also discusses the earlier literature. On Marshall, Edgeworth and wage bargaining see also Hicks (1930).

In discussing the no-profit entrepreneur, Stigler (1941, pp. 127–8) is also misleading when he says that, 'Edgeworth refuses to accept the concept. The apparent reason . . . is that the idea of self-directed . . . production is too heroic a construction to posses any realism'. Schumpeter's discussion is rather odd because on the page following the quotation given in the text he refers to confusion about the no-profit entrepreneur but says, 'with economists' loose ways of expressing themselves, I find it very difficult to array individuals whose statements might be amenable to more favourable interpretations' (1954, p. 1049, n. 59). Schumpeter also accepted that the entrepreneur in Walras's model (as in modern static analysis) was reduced to the role of 'ordinary business routine' (1954, p. 1001, n. 6). He also misrepresents Edgeworth (1954, p. 893, n. 3). As usual, Wicksell (1901, p. 126) has a clear statement of the result. On Wicksteed (1894) Edgeworth also referred to the review by Flux, who first mentioned the importance of Euler's theorem for homogeneous functions; see also the discussion by Baumol and Goldfeld (1968) where the review is reprinted. Edgeworth refused to publish in the *Economic Journal* a review of Wicksteed's book by Barone, much to Walras's annoyance. Robbins (1970, p. 196) suggested that this refusal arose from a fear on Edgeworth's part of offending Marshall. For general discussion of Euler's theorem see Stigler (1941, pp. 320–87). The debate between Wicksteed and Edgeworth is of further interest because of the fact that they are the two main 'disciples' of Jevons, although Wicksteed was much more sympathetic towards Comte, and less sympathetic towards utilitarianism. On Jevons's influence on Wicksteed see Herford (1931, p. 199), who also describes regular economic discussions between 1884 and 1888 (at the house of Henry Beeton) of a circle including Wicksteed, Edgeworth, Foxwell, Sidney Webb, and Bernard Shaw. Other work of Edgeworth's relating to production is his clarification of the laws of returns (1925, ii). This defined average and marginal returns to a variable factor, and examined joint costs, and complements and substitutes in production. This is fairly straightforward, and has been examined at length by Stigler (1941, pp. 122–4).

7

Taxation and International Trade

It has been seen that after 1881 Edgeworth increasingly devoted most of his creative energy to mathematical statistics, although his contribution to economics was still substantial. The style of Edgeworth's output has been discussed in chapter 1, and was well described by Keynes who said that:

> so far from rising from the Monograph to the Treatise, moving to the opposite extreme from Marshall's, he sank from the Monograph to the paper, essay, article, or transaction. For forty years a long stream of splinters split off from his bright mind to illumine (and to obscure) the pages of the *Statistical* and *Economic Journals*. (1972, p. 232)

Edgeworth's further work on exchange and distribution has been examined in the previous chapter, but in the 1890s he produced two surveys of considerable importance. These surveys, of the pure theory of taxation and of the pure theory of international values, were both published in the *Economic Journal* and subsequently reproduced (with alterations) in his *Papers* (1925, vol. ii). Each survey consisted of three separate parts, and displayed a staggering breadth of knowledge and command of the subject. They represent his most serious attempts to produce any kind of synthesis of a branch of economic literature, and he obviously gave much serious thought to the question of arrangement, although the resulting taxonomic approach does not make for easy reading. For example, the taxation paper has been described by Schumpeter in the following terms:

> as usual, his exposition proceeds by what I beg leave to describe as picking out currants . . . so that we have difficulty in visualising the spacious whole that is in fact the peak performance of its field and period. (1954, p. 946)

No attempt will therefore be made to provide a comprehensive review of these survey papers of pure theory; emphasis is given below to those aspects which have been of most interest to later generations. Section 7.1 examines his paper on taxation, concentrating on the so-called 'tax paradox' and his analysis of progressive income taxation. Section 7.2 then briefly discusses his comments on the gains from trade and the optimum tariff; as Edgeworth himself admitted, there was little that was original in his survey of the pure theory of trade although the specialist will find it indispensable.

7.1 The Theory of Taxation

Edgeworth began his survey with the rather strong statement that, 'the science of taxation comprises two subjects to which the character of pure theory may be ascribed; the laws of incidence, and the principle of equal sacrifice (1925, ii, p. 64). He then considered a variety of special cases and contexts of tax incidence (using a 'new classification formed by four dichotomous cross divisions', while monopoly 'presents a bifurcation peculiar to itself'). The basic framework for incidence analysis was the simple partial equilibrium approach, still used in many basic textbooks, in which the incidence depends on the relative values of supply and demand elasticities. Edgeworth's statement is highly characteristic:

> If . . . we represent the undisturbed relation of the parties by the equilibrium of two balls resting against each other in a bowl, it may seem, at first sight, that a wedge inserted between the two balls will raise one of them to the full extent of the thickness of the wedge. But on reflection it is evident that this only occurs in the limiting case when the mass of one ball may be neglected in comparison with that of the other. In the absence of data respecting the relative masses of the balls all we can say is that the distance between them will be equal to the thickness of the interposing lamina. Corresponding to the masses of the two balls are the elasticities of demand and supply for the two parties. The general principle is that the tax inflicts more loss on either party, the less the elasticity of that party's demand or supply; other things, including the other party's elasticity, being the same. (1925, ii, p. 66)

Although the metaphor of the 'wedge' is still often used in discussions of the effects of taxes, it seems likely that the reader would already need to know the point well before appreciating Edgeworth's 'explanation'. The metaphor of two balls in a bowl was perhaps borrowed from Marshall (1890), where it was used in several contexts.

The basic approach to incidence analysis actually stemmed from the important paper by Jenkin (1871). It suggests that in general the price of the taxed good will either remain constant (in the extreme case of inelastic supply) or will increase. However, this result ignores interrelationships among commodities. Edgeworth showed that when such interrelationships are explicitly allowed, there are some circumstances in which the price of the taxed good will actually *fall*. When discussing this 'paradox', Edgeworth reproduced his argument which had in fact been explored in more detail in his paper on monopoly, published in Italian in the same year, 1897. Edgeworth's analysis depended on the concepts of complements and substitutes, which have already been discussed in chapter 6.

The Taxation Paradox

Edgeworth first stated his 'paradox' in the following terms:

> when the supply of two or more correlated commodities – such as the carriage of passengers by rail first class or third class – is in the hands of a single monopolist, a tax on one of the articles – e.g. a percentage of first class fares – may prove advantageous to the consumers as a whole. . . . The fares for *all* the classes might be reduced. (1925, i, p. 139)

Edgeworth regarded this result as an example of a situation where, 'the abstract reasoning serves as a corrective to what has been called the "metaphysical incumbus" of dogmatic *laisser faire*' (1925, i, p. 139; see also 1925, ii, pp. 93–4). Essentially the two commodities must be substitutes or 'rivals' in consumption and production, and the result is partly brought about by the fact that the monopolist has an incentive to increase the supply of the untaxed commodity. Edgeworth also recognized that the result could occur in competitive markets (see 1925, ii, p. 63).

This result was greeted with a certain amount of incredulity. For example, Seligman (1921, p. 214) referred to it as, 'a slip of Mr. Edgeworth' and went on to make fun of it by suggesting that the result, 'will surely be a grateful boon to the perplexed and weary secretaries of the Treasury and ministers of finance throughout the world'. It may seem that as a result of this criticism Edgeworth subsequently took every opportunity he could find to criticize Seligman, but this was mainly because Seligman was without doubt the leading authority on public finance, and Edgeworth in fact had a very high regard for him (see 1925, i, p. 93). Edgeworth was obviously alluding to Seligman when he later wrote that the tax paradox was, 'calculated to excite the derision which was bestowed by an economist of the highest sagacity' (1925, ii, p. 479).

As with many of Edgeworth's original results, this tax paradox was not a subject of continuous development. Its main practical importance perhaps arises from the fact that in the early 1930s it attracted the attention of Hotelling, who consequently produced another of his outstanding and seminal papers (1932). Hotelling showed convincingly the conditions under which the result can occur in competitive and monopolistic markets. It is worth reporting Hotelling's statement that the 'paradoxical discovery . . . is one proposition of economic importance which everyone can appreciate but which cannot be proved, apparently, without the use of formulae; moreover, it is very suggestive of further developments' (quoted by Garver, 1933, p. 402). With regard to the first point, Wicksell (1901, pp. 93–5) had already provided a simplified exposition using only a diagram (see also Wicksell, 1958, p. 108). But there is no doubt about the further developments; Hotelling's analysis led him to show for the first time how restrictions derived from utility theory could be used in the estimation of systems of demand equations, and he applied appropriate tests to some results of Schultz. This led directly to Schultz's important 1933 paper on interrelations of demand, involving criticism of the 'ALEP' concepts of substitutes and complements (as discussed in chapter 6). A related, and much neglected, aspect of Schultz's work will also be discussed in the next chapter.

Income Taxation and Progressivity

The section of the taxation survey which attracted most immediate attention was, however, Edgeworth's discussion of the various 'sacrifice' theories of the distribution of the tax burden, and his qualified support for progressive taxation. Edgeworth's attitude to taxation was very similar to that of the major classical economists in that he rejected a quid pro quo approach, on the argument that taxation is not an economic bargain governed by competition. Thus in his view the problem was to determine, 'the distribution of those taxes which are applied to common purposes, the benefits whereof cannot be allocated to particular classes of citizens' (1925, ii, p. 103). Some principle of justice is thus required, and it has already been seen in chapter 5 that Edgeworth argued, along neo-contractarian lines, that the utilitarian arrangement would be accepted by individuals uncertain of their own prospects and taking an equal a priori view of the probabilities.

Having justified the use of utilitarianism as a principle of distribution justice, Edgeworth then succinctly stated the main argument:

> The condition that the total net utility procured by taxation should be a maximum then reduces to the condition that the total disutility should be a minimum . . . it follows in general that the marginal disutility incurred by each taxpayer should be the same. (1925, ii, p. 103)

The implication is that if all individuals have the same cardinal utility function, after-tax incomes would be equalized. Edgeworth also clearly recognized that if there is considerable dispersion of pre-tax incomes relative to the total amount of tax to be raised, where there is, 'not enough tax to go around' (1925, ii, p. 103), the equi-marginal condition cannot be fully satisfied unless there is a 'negative income tax' which raises the incomes of the poorest individuals to a common level. Thus, 'The *acme* of socialism is for a moment sighted' (1925, ii, p. 104). But Edgeworth immediately considered the practical limitations to such high progressive taxation. The following quotation illustrates one of Edgeworth's favourite metaphors, his respect for Sidgwick, his attitude to authority, his views on utilitarianism and the applicability of pure theory, and of course his unmistakable style:

> In this misty and precipitous region let us take Professor Sidgwick as our chief guide. He best has contemplated the crowning height of the utilitarian first principle, from which the steps of a sublime deduction lead to the high tableland of equality; but he also discerns the enormous interposing chasms which deter practical wisdom from moving directly towards that ideal. (1925, ii, p. 104)

Among the various limitations, Edgeworth noted differences in individual utility functions, population effects, the disincentives to work, growth of 'culture' and knowledge, savings, and of course the problem of evasion. He later provided a long list of questions which should be asked when considering the limits to taxable capacity in any 'concrete case' (see 1925, ii, p. 118). In view of his strong qualifications, Edgeworth's influence on the movement towards progressive income taxation in Britain has often been exaggerated. The excessive influence ascribed to such theoretical discussions also neglects the considerable importance of the increase in the franchise for the political acceptance of redistribution as a legitimate role of government.

As always, Edgeworth was keen to quote an authority for the use of minimum total sacrifice (and hence equal marginal sacrifice) as the appropriate criterion. It is noteworthy that even in *Mathematical Psychics* he referred to Mill's discussion of the 'sacrifice' arising from taxation (see 1881, p. 95, n. 2), but in the 1897 paper he takes pains to suggest that Mill actually advocated the principle of equal *marginal* sacrifice (see 1925, ii, pp. 115–16).

The alternative interpretations of the vague phrase 'equal sacrifice' are of course 'equal absolute sacrifice' and 'equal proportional sacrifice'; both were rejected by Edgeworth. He argued that whereas minimum sacrifice requires only the assumption of diminishing marginal utility to produce the result that income tax should be progressive, much more information about individuals' utility functions is required before the alternatives give any definite prescription. For equal absolute sacrifice, taxes are progressive, proportional or regressive according to whether or not the elasticity of the marginal utility of income is greater, equal to, or less than unity. For equal proportional sacrifice, taxes are progressive if the marginal utility of income schedule is steeper than a rectangular hyperbola. Edgeworth rejected the logarithmic (Bernoulli), or other explicit forms and, for the case of equal proportional sacrifice, later argued that, 'In order to obtain a ratio between two "lots" of satisfaction . . . there is required a precision of hedonic units which few utilitarians would venture to postulate' (1925, ii, p. 235).

Edgeworth later became engaged in yet another controversy with Seligman over the meaning and usefulness of the various sacrifice principles – employing his usual curious mixture of acrimony and excessive politeness. When examining Mill's argument, Edgeworth suggested that, 'equal sacrifice is but a corrupt reading for equi-marginal sacrifice', and 'it may well be doubted whether Mill entertained the notion of proportional sacrifice' (1925, ii, p. 115). After considering Seligman's argument, Edgeworth then said, 'on reconsideration I am disposed to omit the word "well"' (1925, ii, p. 235). The use of minimum sacrifice was soon to become standard in the analysis of taxation. However, the use of an assumption of diminishing marginal utility of *income* was not without its critics. It may also be noted that Edgeworth did suggest a general formula giving 'effectual continual progression' (1925, ii, p. 249). This related pre- and post-tax incomes (x and y respectively) by $y = \alpha x^{\beta}$. Nevertheless, to the practical question of, 'exactly where you should tighten or no' he replied, 'that is beyond my science' (1925, ii, p. 260).

The later work on 'optimal taxation', from Mirrlees (1971) onwards, may also be viewed as an exercise in examining in rigorous terms the implications for taxation of adopting alternative principles of distributive justice. In this sense it can be regarded as a direct descendant of Edgeworth, and in addition much of the work uses the calculus of variations which was familiar to Edgeworth. However, the optimal tax literature of more recent years is distinguished by the explicit inclusion of the possible incentive effects (mainly relating to labour supply) of taxation. Furthermore, it has clearly demonstrated the considerable sensitivity of the implied tax structure to assumptions about the precise form of the utility function.

An important point to notice about Edgeworth's analysis of the pure theory of taxation arises clearly from his work on the minimum sacrifice theory. His approach can be seen as marking a crucial stage in the transition towards a 'welfare economics' view of public finance, rather than using a special set of 'tax maxims' such as the famous criteria laid down by Adam Smith.

7.2 International Values

The Gains from Trade

Edgeworth's survey of the pure theory of international values was in some ways responsible for a change of emphasis in the approach to trade theory, despite the fact that it contained few original analytical contributions. Indeed, he said that, 'Mill's exposition of the general theory is still unsurpassed' (1925, ii, p. 20), and acknowledged further that, 'what is written . . . after a perusal of

[Marshall's] privately circulated chapters . . . can make no claim to originality' (1925, ii, p. 46). Not surprisingly Edgeworth was largely concerned to bring the 'province' of trade theory under the suzerainty of 'Mathematical Psychics'.

He began: 'International trade meaning in plain English trade between nations, it is not surprising that the term should mean something else in political economy' (1925, ii, p. 5). The defining characteristic was of course the immobility of factors of production, but for Edgeworth:

> The fundamental principle of international trade is that general theory . . . the Theory of Exchange . . . which . . . constitutes the 'kernel' of most of the chief problems in economics. It is a corollary of the general theory that all the parties to a bargain look to gain by it . . . This is the generalised statement of the theory of comparative cost. (1925, ii, p. 6)

Thus the gains from trade are analogous to the gains from exchange in simple barter and, 'It is useful . . . to contemplate the theory of distribution as analogous to that of international trade proper' (1925, ii, p. 19). Hence trade theory is to Edgeworth simply one more application of the general method of 'Mathematical Psychics'. This type of emphasis came to dominate much of the later analysis in the pure theory of international trade. Indeed, many modern students will have more experience of handling Edgeworth box diagrams in the context of trade theory than in some conventional courses in microeconomics.

One of Edgeworth's criticisms of Mill (1848) was that the latter took as his measure of the gain from trade the change in the ratio of exchange of exports against imports. Thus Mill in this case 'confounds "final" with integral utility' (1925, ii, p. 22). The same point had in fact been made by Jevons (1957, pp. 154–6). However, Edgeworth, while preferring total utility, admitted that Mill was not otherwise led to serious error in using his own measure.

In directly applying the theory of exchange to that of trade, there are two points worth noting about Edgeworth's use of offer curves. First he was quite content to use community indifference curves without clearly specifying how aggregation might be carried out. He said only that, 'By combining properly the utility curves for all the individuals, we obtain what may be called a collective utility curve' (1925, ii, p. 293). Secondly he fully anticipated Graham's (1923) later criticism of the use of offer curves by stating that:

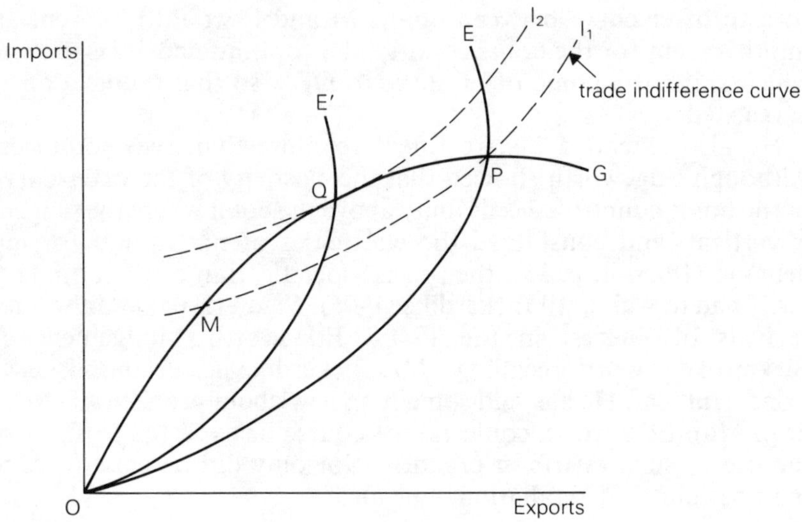

Figure 7.1 The optimum tariff

> A movement along a supply-and-demand curve of international trade should be considered as attended with rearrangements of internal trade; as the movements of the hands of a clock correspond to considerable unseen movements of the machinery. (1925, ii, p. 32)

Edgeworth's survey was, as always, extremely wide ranging, though for later developments the most interesting parts are concerned with his elucidation of Mill's 'recognition of the case in which an impediment may be beneficial – or an improvement prejudicial – to one of the countries' (1925, ii, p. 9). These two cases would now be discussed under the headings of the 'optimal tariff' and (following Bhagwati, 1958) 'immiserising growth', the first of which is discussed briefly below.

The Optimum Tariff

Edgeworth's analysis of the optimum tariff (1925, ii, p. 39) was similar to that of, 'Auspitz and Lieben's beautiful and original reasoning' (1925, ii, p. 295). The basic geometry is shown in figure 7.1, where the initial home and foreign offer curves are shown by OE and OG respectively. The initial home trade indifference curve is I_1, and a movement to any position along the foreign offer curve between points M and P would represent an improvement for the home country. The optimum tariff is the one which shifts the home offer curve to OE′, so that point Q on I_2 is reached.

He also extended his treatment to more than two countries. Although Edgeworth showed that the elasticity of the offer curve of the home country exceeds unity above the point where the tangent is vertical, and considered the elasticities of native and foreign demand (1925, ii, p. 35), the precise specification of the optimum tariff had to wait until Bickerdike (1906), Pigou (1908) and the later revivals of interest in the 1940s. Edgeworth's judgement of Bickerdike is worth recalling: 'Mr. Bickerdike has accomplished a wonderful feat. He has said something new about protection' (1925, ii, p. 344). Edgeworth could not of course be expected to support the use of such tariffs in practice. Not only did he acknowledge the possibility of retaliation, but also:

> For one nation to benefit itself at the expense of . . . others is contrary to the highest morality . . . But in an abstract study upon the motion of projectiles *in vacuo*, I do not think it necessary to enlarge upon the horrors of war. (1925, ii, p. 17, n. 5)

The 'highest morality' was, of course, the principal of utilitarianism.

Further Reading

On the 'Edgeworth taxation paradox' there is also Garver's (1933) comment on Hotelling's (1932) paper, and the latter's reply (1933). Bailey (1954) later showed the conditions under which the phenomenon could be 'one way'; that is, may occur when one of the monopolized goods is taxed but not the other. In a volume of papers in honour of Hotelling, further analyses were carried out by Vickrey (1958) and Ferguson (1958). See also Baumol and Goldfeld (1968, p. 190). On minimum sacrifice, Edgeworth was firmly supported by Pigou who argued that, 'there can be no question that . . . least aggregate sacrifice is an ultimate principle of sacrifice' (1947, p. 43). For further discussion and criticisms see Shehab (1953), Blum and Kalven (1953), Fagan (1938) and Schumpeter (1954, p. 1071). For general discussion of Edgeworth's taxation analysis see Doresamienger (1929), and for historical perspective see Creedy (1984a). For the conditions on utility functions required for progressivity with alternative criteria, see Pigou (1947, p. 89) and Musgrave (1959, pp. 98–102). Edgeworth (1925, ii, p. 269) also considered the special case of a tax schedule where $y = x^{\beta}$. Ironically, this schedule arises from the application of equal proportional sacrifice, with a logarithmic utility function, two assumptions of which Edgeworth did not approve. For $u = \log x$ and a tax rate $t(x)$, the loss of utility s, is equal to $-\log[1 - t(x)]$, and for constant $s/u = k$, then $t(x) = 1 - x^{-k}$ and $y = x^{1-k}$. In considering Edgeworth's controversies with Seligman it is worth noting that elsewhere he quoted the 'Miltonic' rule for selecting an adversary: 'Best with the best, more glory will be won, or less be lost' (1925, ii, p. 282).

In his trade survey Edgeworth also retracted his criticism of Bastable and Pigou concerning the symmetry of import and export taxes; see also Pigou (1947, p. 180), and the detailed treatment of this issue by Lerner (1936). Edgeworth regarded Mill's 'supplement' as 'laborious and confusing' but for a contrary view see Schumpeter (1954, p. 608, n. 7). On Edgeworth's use of offer curves in trade analysis it may be noted that Viner (1964, p. 546) criticizes Edgeworth's diagram (1925, ii, p. 32) for not including a straight line section in each offer curve to cover the situations where the country does not trade. However, Edgeworth's axes refer to exports and imports, and not to exportables and importables. Viner also interprets the phrase 'to generalise the theory' as meaning to allow for non-constant returns to scale (1964, p. 547, n. 24), but this does not seem appropriate. On the use of indifference curves here see Leontief (1933). On optimum tariffs and retaliation, along with references to the 1940s literature, see Johnson (1953). Finally, a useful general review of the contemporary *Economic Journal* literature on trade and public finance is included in Jha (1973).

8

Conclusion

8.1 Central Themes

It has been seen that Edgeworth did not begin working and writing in economics until his mid thirties, but in common with the vast majority of neoclassical economists he soon pursued an academic career as a professor of economics. Indeed, in a period which saw the rapid and widespread professionalization of the subject, Edgeworth held an academic position in England which was regarded as second only to that of Alfred Marshall. Furthermore, and in spite of his wide range of reading and sympathies, Edgeworth's work was characterized by the fact that it was virtually all addressed to his fellow professional economists. So uncompromising was he in his view that economics is a very difficult subject which offers only very remote (and nearly always negative) advice to the policy maker, that it may fairly be said that his work was addressed to just a small number of 'fellow travellers' in the rarefied atmosphere of the 'higher regions' of pure theory. However, Edgeworth imposed no geographical limitations, and with his considerable linguistic skills and international sympathies was in contact with the majority of leading economists around the world; this aspect will be discussed further in section 8.2.

Contract: Exchange and Distribution

One purpose of this book has been to emphasize a major thread which runs through all Edgeworth's work in economics, and that is his emphasis on the problem of distribution. It has been seen in chapter 2 how his wide background in science and literature, with the strong utilitarian influence, informed his early writings on 'methods of ethics'. His mathematical analysis of the implications of utilitarianism for the optimal distribution was not only highly original (and esoteric) but laid the foundation for his work in economics. Thus, as shown in chapters 3 and 5, the transition from *New and Old Methods of Ethics* to *Mathematical Psychics* was not a shift in major preoccupations but rather a change of emphasis. Distribution was then seen as an important concomitant of exchange, so that the analysis of *contract* became for Edgeworth the central problem. The majority of Edgeworth's original contributions to economics can be seen to involve the twin subjects of exchange and distribution, treated mathematically.

A crucial aspect of Edgeworth's analysis of contract, which has been stressed in this book (especially in chapter 5), is the development of a 'social contract' argument in favour of the use of the utilitarian principle as a principle of social justice. It was surely the realization of this new justification of utilitarianism, using the newly developed analysis of contract, which generated the excitement that is clearly evident in his first work in economics.

Mathematical Psychics

Although it was his first book in economics, and used previously published material, Edgeworth's *Mathematical Psychics* must be regarded as his most complete and original single piece of work. The application of mathematics to the social and moral sciences, with the division into the economical and utilitarian calculus, is a theme which runs strongly, often passionately, throughout the book. The excitement of Edgeworth's discovery of a further justification for utilitarianism, as a principle of arbitration acceptable in social contract terms to all parties, dominates almost every section. The integration of his analysis of barter, and the effects of the introduction of additional traders into the market, with the demonstration that the utilitarian arrangement prescribes a point on the contract curve of efficient exchanges, was to Edgeworth nothing short of 'momentous'.

The analysis was admitted to be highly abstract, and in many places of 'negative' value (clarifying what cannot be achieved); but it was no less important for that. It is interesting to note that his discussion of the value of these abstract results uses almost the same type of argument as the now rather hackneyed statement made by Keynes at the end of his *General Theory* (1936, pp. 383–4). Edgeworth stated:

> Considerations so abstract it would of course be ridiculous to fling upon the flood-tide of practical politics . . . it is at a height of abstraction in the rarefied atmosphere of speculation that the secret springs of action take their rise, and a direction is imparted to the pure foundation of youthful enthusiasm whose influence will ultimately affect the broad current of events. (1881, p. 128)

The intellectual pleasure derived from being able to draw together so many different subjects of analysis, and strands of his enormous range of learning, is clearly evident. However, it is precisely this wide field of vision, combined of course with the technical level and style of writing, which made the book so difficult for his contemporaries, and which continues to make the book seem so strange to the modern reader. For anyone wishing to read *Mathematical Psychics* an appendix has been added to this book which provides some 'labour saving' guidance. Emphasis has been given to this book, so often quoted but so seldom read, because it really provides the key to all his work.

The central theme of Edgeworth's work is also clear in his revealing statement, taken from his 1889 Presidential address to Section F of the Royal Society, that:

> It may be said that in pure economics there is only one fundamental theorem, but that is a very difficult one: the theory of bargain in a wide sense. The direct application of mathematical reasoning is . . . limited – more limited, I think, than the corresponding function of the higher statistics. (1925, ii, p. 288)

This quotation is of interest not only for its clear statement about pure theory, but also for its explicit view about the relative roles of mathematics and statistics. Edgeworth's views concerning the role of mathematics in economics have been discussed in chapter 1, and the point has been stressed that he was always extremely cautious about the application of results in pure theory to economic policy problems. It must always be remembered that a very large proportion of Edgeworth's energy was devoted to work in mathematical statistics. Most of his publications during the 1880s were on statistical subjects (including index numbers), and even after his appointment to the Drummond Chair at Oxford, and the editorship of the *Economic Journal*, he published mainly in statistical journals. However, and as Bowley (1934, p. 21) pointed out: 'to Edgeworth there was an underlying unity in the fundamental conceptions and in much of the method of economics and statistics'.

The difference between Marshall and Edgeworth in the use of mathematics in their publications is so obvious that it may be all too easy to exaggerate the difference between their attitudes to the role of pure theory. The above quotation from Edgeworth in 1889 may be compared with the following statement made to Edgeworth in a letter from Marshall of 1902:

> I conceive no more calamitous notion than that abstract, or general, or 'theoretical' economics was 'economics' proper. It seems to me an essential but very small part of economics proper: and by itself sometimes even – well, not a very good occupation of time. (in Pigou, ed., 1925a, p. 437)

While Edgeworth may have accepted the first part of Marshall's statement, it seems unlikely that he would have agreed with the final sentiment. Indeed, in his inaugural lecture at Oxford in 1891, Edgeworth offered the following advice:

> The margin of profit and loss in the intellectual . . . world will differ with the personality of individuals. No general rule is available except that, like the cultivated Athenian, we should eschew the invidious comparison of each others' pursuits. (1925, i, p. 11)

8.2 Later Perspectives

It has been seen that Edgeworth's books and articles in economics were written in an uncompromising style, and his analysis was often far from transparent. But in considering later views of his work and major contributions, care must be taken not to exaggerate this aspect. After all, he did not publish in obscure journals, and his major work, *Mathematical Psychics*, was initially well reviewed and often referred to by leading economists. It is important to recognize, as mentioned several times in this book, that the major preoccupations of Edgeworth were quite representative of those of his contemporaries. Edgeworth's style was without doubt highly idiosyncratic, but the major difficulties for the modern reader are raised by the fact that the current general view of 'neoclassical economics' does not correspond exactly with what was being said by the leading economists of the neoclassical period.

There seems little doubt that the modern perspective is somewhat distorted by a general neglect of the work of Edgeworth's contemporaries, and by the use of a framework of analysis largely affected by theoretical work dating from the 1930s. As argued in the Introduction to this book, a great deal of work remains to be done on the neoclassical period, and this limited study of Edgeworth is written in that spirit. Edgeworth may have suffered relative neglect, and his work involves special difficulties, but in this context it is worth repeating the complaint made by Hutchison, concerning the least neglected economist, that:

> A considerable part . . . of the fulsome tributes to Marshall paid by his immediate successors had an element of lip service about them, while some of his most fundamental ideas and interests were being quietly abandoned. (1981, p. 47)

For many years Edgeworth's analysis of the recontracting process was largely ignored, and his indifference curves were used mainly as just a part of the pure theory of demand. In text book discussions of, for example, income and substitution effects, Edgeworth is sometimes given credit for 'inventing' indifference curves, but then more often than not it is then pointed out that this 'ironically' paved the way for the abandonment of a cardinal concept of utility. To view the innovation of indifference curves simply as a component of demand analysis is really to ignore Edgeworth's main emphasis on distribution in *Mathematical Psychics*.

As shown earlier, he argued that with few competitors there would be indeterminacy in the rate of exchange, so that the analysis cannot proceed using demand curves, and arbitration would be required involving the use of a principle of distributive justice and explicit interpersonal comparisons. The demonstration that the utilitarian arrangement would (under specified conditions) be acceptable to egoistic individuals, placing them on the contract curve, was for Edgeworth one of his major results. The further result that a large number of competitors would, by recontracting, reach a final settlement that is equivalent to the price-taking position was also very important, but Edgeworth stressed that it would not necessarily be the utilitarian arrangement. This point, along with emphasis on the widespread existence of indeterminacy in practice, was important in his criticism of dogmatic *laissez faire* attitudes. It is a serious distortion to argue, as some later commentators have, that the neoclassical economists were uncritical supporters of *laissez faire* policy. But of course this has long been a favourite caricature of popular critics of economics.

It is useful to recognize that later perspectives are affected by the significant changes in the types of economic problem, and the attitudes of economists towards policy, from the late 1920s and the 1930s. A negligible amount of what Edgeworth and his contemporaries wrote can be described as 'macroeconomics'. During the last part of the nineteenth century the 'value and distribution' theories of the classical economists were abandoned, but, as Hutchison (1981, p. 236) has pointed out, 'the self equilibrating macroeconomics for a short time survived unscathed'. All this was to change in the 1930s, just a few years after nearly all the leading economists of Edgeworth's generation had died (see the Introduction to this book).

The 1930s may perhaps be described as a 'decade of controversies' conducted within a group of younger professional economists who had entered directly into the subject, rather than approaching it at a more mature age from other disciplines. Furthermore, a much wider role for government economic policy was more generally accepted. Despite the 'moral fervour' of so many late Victorian economists, their role in policy debates was very different indeed from that of the next generation.

Reaction Against Utilitarianism

There is also little doubt that the modern view of Edgeworth's contribution is significantly affected by the reaction against utilitarianism, and by a rather narrow view of Edgeworth's own approach to it. It is now quite common for reviewers of the period to repeat Hutchison's summary statement that:

> What was important in marginal utility was the adjective rather than the noun. Marginal utility analysis introduced the marginal concept as an instrument of maximisation analysis. 'Utility' was only for a brief period to have any substantial or unchallenged role in economic theory. (1953, p. 16)

This must, however, be regarded as a rather extreme view. Indeed, economics has not yet managed to dispense with cardinal utility in many areas. It is used in a great deal of empirical work in demand analysis, in addition to pure theory. Even Fisher and Pareto were both unable to dispense with cardinal utility in some of their writings. As Edgeworth and others argued, interpersonal comparisons cannot be avoided in many contexts, and economists have in practice not been willing to accept the narrow confines which rejection implies. Furthermore the Pareto criterion, that a gain for any individual, whatever the relative income position, is viewed as an improvement only so long as no one becomes worse off, is regarded by many as itself a value judgement though it was initially used as the basis of the 'new' welfare economics. The analysis of the implications for policy of explicitly stated value judgements is of course a widely accepted and important role of economic theory.

The initial reaction against utilitarianism was not primarily based on methodological grounds, but the later emphasis on 'testing', by strong falsificationists, also led to criticisms. For example, in what is still the most valuable book on the neoclassical period, Hutchison was strongly criticial of Edgeworth's remarks concerning the utilitarian arrangement and the contract curve. He argued that such statements are 'intolerably ambiguous' and:

> any meaning that might reasonably be attached to them would, as far as one ever could test it, be very trivial. We cannot attempt here to boil away the steaming metaphysical fluids in Edgeworth's saucepan and weigh up, or 'extricate', the possibly unimpressive and uninteresting crystal of attestable fact that one may guess is all that would eventually be discoverable. (1953, p. 111)

The emphasis on 'facts' and empirical 'tests' in this statement should be noted of course. It is surely not necessary to be a strong supporter of Edgeworth in order to argue that the use of the words 'trivial' and 'unimpressive' are somewhat extreme.

In view of the nature of many of the criticisms by economists against utilitarianism, the feelings of the 'Edgeworthite cardinalist deviationist', Robertson, about interpersonal comparisons is perhaps not surprising. He wrote:

> I am never quite sure whether one must not try to do this because it is impossible, and attempting the impossible is a wicked waste of time; or because, while perfectly possible, the process is held to involve making judgements about what is nice or nasty, and not simply about what is true or untrue. (1952, p. 37)

Robertson found it 'very hard not to get cross' (1952, p. 39) when being told that cardinal utility is redundant, not because he did not appreciate the simple analysis of consumer demand, but because he, like Edgeworth and Marshall, felt that such 'important matters as taxation policy' (1952, p. 38) should also be part of the legitimate sphere of analysis of the economist. Despite enormous practical problems, 'there is no difficulty . . . about *stating* the problem in terms of the utilitarian calculus' (1952, p. 40). This subject is really much too large to be discussed adequately here. But it is hoped that enough has been said in this book to show that the statement (by Schumpeter, quoted earlier), that economics can easily dispense with Edgeworth's utilitarianism without affecting its 'scientific content', is a gross oversimplification.

The International Flow of Ideas

Another factor affecting modern perspectives on the work of Edgeworth and his contemporaries concerns the international flow of ideas, or more specifically the insularity of British economics after the middle 1920s. Following the lead set by Jevons, the late 1880s and 1890s can be regarded as the 'high period' in the international exchange of ideas. As Hutchison stated: 'Edgeworth, Wicksteed, Auspitz and Lieben, Wieser, Böhm-Bawerk, Wicksell, Walras, Pareto, Barone and Fisher all drew on a broad, internationally known literature' (1955, p. 9).

Important and original works were, 'constructed essentially on the basis of a wide, eclectic, cosmopolitan reading of their contemporaries and immediate predecessors' (Hutchison, 1955, p. 9). All this was to change very rapidly, and soon after the turn of the century there was a considerable reduction in the international flow of ideas. Even by 1901, Ely complained to Marshall that, 'I could wish that there were a closer connection between American economists and English economists, but I am not sure how strong the desire for this closer connection may be on the part of your people' (in Coats, 1961, p. 122). Ely went on to make the telling observation that there was a closer connection between German and American writers, than between the latter and English writers.

Of relevance to the present study, Hutchison (1955, p. 10) also makes the interesting point that, despite Edgeworth's international sympathies, publications by non-English economists in the *Economic Journal* were negligible. Furthermore, the *Journal* played no part in securing translations of major works, and it seems that the only translation which Edgeworth encouraged was that of Pierson's *Principles* (1902). However, with his linguistic skills, Edgeworth may not have recognized a general need for translations. The lack of foreign authors may perhaps be explained by the dominance of Marshall (in which Edgeworth fully acquiesced) and a desire not to burden the pages of the *Journal* with esoteric debates about pure theory. However, there is a sharp contrast with the much more cosmopolitan interests shown in contemporary issues of the American *Quarterly Journal of Economics*, which in other ways provided the model for the *Economic Journal*.

There is little doubt that the charge of insularity applies to British economists, and not to American and European writers. Ekelund and Hébert (1983, p. 325, n. 5) do not exaggerate when they say that, 'insularity, if not downright chauvinism, again characterized British economic thought'. The case of Cambridge is of course notorious (see, for example, Johnson and Johnson, 1978, p. 221; Hutchison, 1981, p. 47), but in Britain the personal example set by Robbins in encouraging colleagues at the London School of Economics to read more widely is a rare exception to the charge. In discussing the extensive *Review of Economic Theory* by Cannan, Viner (1958, p. 396) complained of the fact that, 'of non-English economists there is but scanty attention'.

This characteristic is particularly unfortunate in view of the importance of the work being ignored. In the present context, the valuable contributions of Hotelling should especially be mentioned and, as shown in chapter 7, his early work was significantly influenced by Edgeworth. The published work of Hotelling, and other mathematical economists working in America, such as Evans, Roos, Wald, Morgenstern and Von Neumann, was largely ignored in Britain. These may perhaps be described as a 'first generation' of American economists with advanced training in mathematics. Drawing on a wide range of sources, like Edgeworth they used their techniques to make significant progress in economic theory, but unfortunately they had a negligible impact on the development of British economic thought.

The rare excursions of British economists into overseas literature tended not to correct the insularity, but instead to present a rather narrow view of their subject. Consider, for example, the complaint of Wold and Jureen that:

> the present tendencies to nationalise science do not make for better understanding. A habit seems to be on the increase to

> regard foreign literature as *terra incognita*, the contributions of which it is a merit to 'rediscover'. (1953, p. 323)

There seems little doubt that Wold would have had in mind the 'rediscovery' of the work of Pareto and Slutsky by Hicks and Allen in the 1930s. In fact, this celebrated work resulted in a significant over-estimation of the originality of Pareto, and a neglect of the works of, for example, Fisher, Johnson, and other Europeans discussed in this book. It is instructive to compare this 'rediscovery' with the approach of the scholarly American Schultz. Hotelling pointed out that Schultz studied the work of Cournot, Edgeworth, Cassel, Walras, and other mathematical economists thoroughly, and that:

> he pointed out the important work of Slutsky . . . His discovery of this previously ignored work of Slutsky is an instance of the wide dragnet with which he sought out original ideas from all sources (1939, p. 991).

Hotelling's statement suggests that Schultz had priority in the 'rediscovery', and it is interesting to see that Schultz only quietly mentioned this in a footnote to his great work (1938, p. 38, n. 42), where the similar independent discovery by Valentino Dominedo was also noted. With such different attitudes to scholarship, it is not surprising that the names of Schultz and Dominedo are hardly ever mentioned in connection with the 'rediscovery' of Slutsky's work.

The reasons for and consequences of British insularity, from the period after Edgeworth and his contemporaries, raises many interesting issues which cannot be discussed further here. Even with the vastly improved communication between countries, and the dominance of the English (American) language in economic literature, more modern examples may easily be cited (see, for example, Prest, 1979, p. 245, n. 2). But it may be appropriate to conclude with the thought that economics has generally become more 'narrow' in its approach, not so much in a national sense but in terms of the perspective which is brought to the analysis of economic issues. The difference between the outlook of the late Victorians and that of more recent generations of economists is brought into sharp focus by reading the work of Edgeworth. It is therefore hoped that this book can provide a little help in gaining a better understanding of the neoclassical economists although, as mentioned earlier, much work remains to be done on the major writers of the period. However, it seems unlikely that much progress will be made so long as the reading of earlier and broader literature remains the province solely of 'specialist' researchers in the history of economic thought.

Further Reading

Virtually every paper by Hotelling on economics proved to be of seminal importance, but special mention may be made of his 1938 'general welfare' paper. For further details of the work of Evans and Roos, see for example, Evans (1930). On von Neumann and Wald see Baumol and Goldfeld (1968). The neglect of the fundamental work of Wald and others working in America was strongly noted in Morgenstern's (1941) article length review of Hicks (1939). Morgenstern complained of the, 'almost complete lack of references to other writings' and of problems arising when:

> . . . a work of this kind is interspersed with frequent claims as to the originality of the thought, when it is so easy to show that many of the seemingly newest ideas have been developed at length elsewhere and when the use of some apparently neglected literature might have prevented the inclusion of statements which are clearly wholly untenable and which have been disproved completely. (1941, pp. 363–4)

Despite the fact that Morgenstern's paper appeared in a major journal, it has been largely ignored, at least in Britain.

Appendix

Notes on *Mathematical Psychics*

A number of difficulties face the modern reader of *Mathematical Psychics*. First, there are very many, brief and often inaccurate, references to other authors, covering a very wide range of literature. The following notes provide, as briefly as possible, some details which may hopefully save the reader a great deal of trouble. Secondly, Edgeworth often used Greek, and occasionally Latin, in the middle of difficult and allusive arguments. Translations of these phrases are given below; these were kindly provided by Oliver Dickinson of the University of Durham. Thirdly, Edgeworth often quoted, obviously from memory, short passages from English literature; but invariably the sources are not given. Most of these quotations have been traced, and are also indicated in the following notes.

Edgeworth also made several notes and corrections to his own copy of *Mathematical Psychics*, now deposited in the library of the London School of Economics. These notes are reproduced below. Other misprints, not noticed by Edgeworth, are also indicated. Furthermore, the third part of *Mathematical Psychics* (pp. 56–82) consists of his 1879 paper in *Mind*, with a number of minor changes. These changes are also noted below.

Where a book or article has already been referred to in the present book, the usual method is employed of giving only the date, and full details are given in the separate list of references. Otherwise information is given in the relevant note. In order to facilitate easy reference the first number of each note is the page number of *Mathematical Psychics*, and the line or footnote number is then given in parentheses. Thus 10(15) refers to page 10, line 15; similarly 10(n. 1) refers to note 1 on page 10.

v(17) Edgeworth used the 2nd edition (1877) of Sidgwick's *Methods of Ethics* (1874).

vi(9) Sidgwick, H. (1879) The Wages Fund Theory, *Fortnightly Review*.

vii(14) For Sidgwick's proof see *Methods of Ethics*, Book IV, Chapter 11.

vii(n. 1) This refers to Edgeworth (1879).

viii(6) 'Someone ignorant of geometry'. The last letter should be ς rather than ι. Plato's Academy forbade entrance to the ἀγεωμετϱητὸς. This word also appears on pp. 3, 83, 95, 117 of *Mathematical Psychics*.

1(n. 1) From p. 96 it is clear that Edgeworth used the 2nd edition (1879) of Jevons's *Theory of Political Economy* (1871). The reference is to the section on 'capability of Exact Measurement' in chapter 1. Compare Edgeworth's introduction here to that of *Metretike* (1887), where he quotes Jevons in the same context.

2(n. 1) Mill, J. S. *A System of Logic*, 2 vols., (1843, 8th edition 1872). The reference to Auguste Comte (1798–1857), the founder of Positivism, is to *Cours de Philosophie Positive*, 6 vols, (1839–42). The reference to Mill's *logic* is probably to Book III, chapter XXIV § 9 (which Edgeworth refers to later, at p. 84) where Mill mentions Comte's *Cours*.

2(n. 1) This review of Jevons's *Theory* is the untitled and anonymous review in the *Saturday Review*, (11 Nov. 1871), discussed in chapter 3.

2(n. 1) This is *Researches sur les Principes Mathematiques de la Theories des Richesses* (1838, translated by N. T. Bacon, with an introduction by I. Fisher in 1897) by Antoine Augustin Cournot (1801–77).

4(n. 3) Professor Sir William Thomson (1824–1907), later Lord Kelvin, and Professor P. G. Tait (1831–1901), *Treatise on Natural Philosophy* (2nd edition 1879). At the age of 22 Kelvin was appointed to the chair of Natural Philosophy at Glasgow, which he held until retiring in 1899 (three times refusing the Cavendish Chair). Peter Guthrie Tait was Professor of mathematics at Belfast (1854–60) and later Professor of Natural Philosophy at Edinburgh 1860–1901.

5(23) The reference to Alfred Marshall (1842–1924) is to the *Pure Theory of Foreign Trade and The Pure Theory of Domestic Values*, privately printed in 1879 by Sidgwick, reprinted in Whitaker (ed.) (1975).

5(24) *Elements of Pure Economics* (1874) by Marie-Esprit Léon Walras (1843–1910); cited below as *Elements*. All page references below are to the English translation by Jaffé (1954).

5(26) William Thomas Thornton (1813–80); see also chapter 3.

5(n. 1) The reference is to Sir George Stokes's *Mathematical and Physical Papers* (1845); see also chapter 2.

6(n. 1) Joseph Louis Francois Bertrand (1822–1900) is the French mathematician, whose (1883) review of Cournot and Walras was quoted by Edgeworth in his paper on monopoly; see chapter 5. Bertrand edited the *Journal des Savants* from 1865.

6(n. 1) Henry William Watson (1827–1903) and Samuel Hawksley Burbury (1831–1911). Edgeworth's reference is to their joint book, *A Treatise on Generalised Co-ordinates applied to the Kinetics of a Material System* (1879).

6(n. 3) Sir Isaac Todhunter (1820–84). The reference is to *Researches in the Calculus of Variations* (1871), which won the Adams' Prize at Cambridge.

7(n. 2) Jevons actually said 'Utility may be treated as a quantity of *two dimensions*, one dimension consisting in the quantity of the commodity, and another in the intensity of the effect produced upon the consumer' (1957, p. 47).

7(n. 3) The reference to Wilhelm Max Wundt (1832–1920) is to his *Grundzüge der Physiologischen Psychologie* (1874). Wundt set up the first psychology laboratory, in Leipzig in 1879, and the first journal for experimental studies, the *Philosophische Studien*, in 1881.

7(n. 4) The reference to Marquis Pierre-Simon de Laplace (1794–1827) is to *Essai Philosophique sur les Probabilités* (1814).

9(27) From Alexander Pope's 'Essay on Man', Epistle I, line 6.

11(1) The mathematician and scientist, W. R. Hamilton (1805–65); see chapter 2.

12(5) The sociologist Herbert Spencer (1820–1903); see also the note to p. 51.

12(n. 1) The reference is to J. S. Mill, *Three Essays on Religion: Nature, the Utility of Religion and Theism* (with Introduction by Helen Taylor, 1874).

12(n. 3) The mathematician Joseph-Louis Lagrange (1736–1813).

13(15) George Henry Lewes (1817–78), English Comtist, editor of the *Fortnightly Review*, and 'husband' of George Eliot.

13(n. 1) James Clerk-Maxwell (1831–79) who became the first Professor of Experimental Physics at Cambridge in 1871. The reference is to *Treatise on Electricity and Magnetism* (1873).

14(n. 3) Balfour Steward (1828–87), director of Kew observatory, and Professor of Natural Philosophy at Owen's College, Manchester.

15(9) Edgeworth changed this to 'an exact social science' in his copy.

15(16) 'The cold blood about my heart would prevent me from being able to follow instinct without these parts'.

16(3) See *Methods of Ethics*, Book II chapter 1, and especially Book IV chapter 1, pp. 411–13.

16(10) 'Compoundedness'.

16(19) This should read 'nor yet'. The effects of introducing sympathy are discussed later by Edgeworth on p. 53; see chapter 4.

17(10) From Alfred Tennyson's 'Maud; A Monodrama', Part I verse II (and again at verse XII).

17(14) Edgeworth changed this to, 'Thus an auctioneer having been in virtual contract with the last bidder . . .' in his copy.

19(16) In his copy Edgeworth added the sentence, 'In the general field, there is usually the condition that each individual should sell only one article'.

19(25) In his copy Edgeworth changed this to, 'when there may be an indefinite number'.

19(n. 1) This reference is to the section on 'Failure of the equations of exchange' (chapter IV), where Jevons discusses book and house sales (1957, pp. 118–27).

20(5) 'to prevent' should read 'to be present'.

20(25) The function $F(xy)$ should be written as $F(x, y)$.

22(n. 2) This is Jevons's section on 'Symbolic statement of the Theory' (1957, p. 99).

22(22) Edgeworth writes the total derivative as DP, which was standard notation at the time.

23(27) The first term should read

$$\left(\frac{d\mathrm{P}}{dy}\right)$$

24(27) The words 'the by' should read 'thereby'.

26(20) The discussion of unstable equilibria in Walras to which Edgeworth refers is probably Part II, lesson 7 § 66–8

(*Elements*, pp. 109–13). The reference here is to the English translation.

26(28) The use of determinants here is discussed in chapter 2.

28 (Fig. 1) The coordinates marked $y_0\xi_0$, $y_2\xi_2$ etc. are later referred to in the text as $\xi_0 y_0$ etc. The lines from the origin to the point marked $\eta\xi$ on the contract curve are not indifference curves, but demand (offer) curves, which are not defined by Edgeworth until later. The points printed as $X'y'$ and $\eta_0 X$ should read $x'y'$ and $\eta_0 x_0$.

29(17) 'Increasing strife and disturbance'.

29(22) 'fighting face to face'.

30(26) Catallactics is a neologism of Richard Whately (1787–1863), who succeeded Senior as Drummond Professor of Political Economy at Oxford 1829–31.

30(n. 1) This again refers to Jevons's section on 'Failure of the Equations of exchange' (1957, p. 124). The word 'mainly' was omitted from this quotation (between 'bargaining' and 'consists') and several commas were added by Edgeworth.

30(n. 2) The book by J. G. Courcelle-Seneuil (1813–92) is actually *Traité Théorique et Practique d'économie Politique* (2nd edition, 1867).

31(2) 'One shape with many names'.

31(n. 1) This refers to Jevons's statement of the 'law of indifference', but his discussion of the 'Definition of Trading Body' is also relevant.

32(2) In his copy Edgeworth changed this to, 'the demands of the entrepreneur are deducible'.

32(n. 2) The corresponding reference to the English translation is to part IV, lesson 18 § 179 (*Elements*, p. 225).

33(8) The phrase 'so there is *a priori* ground', should read, 'so it is not shown by Mr. Sidgwick that there is no *a priori* ground'. Edgeworth noted the correction in his copy.

33(n. 3) Edgeworth deleted this footnote in his copy.

35(29) In his copy Edgeworth added, 'E.g. one competing railway competing with another can offer for the double custom terms much lower than for the single!'

36(9) It may initially seem that one of the indifference curves in Figure 1 is drawn as slightly concave over a section beyond the point $y_0\xi_0$, but it is part of a curve for the other individual.

36(12) There is no point marked $y_1\xi_1$ on Figure 1, but this is obviously slightly north-west of $y_0\xi_0$.

36(20) The denominator of the right-hand term should read

$$F'_y\left(\frac{x'}{2}\frac{y'}{2}\right)$$

37(15) The numerator of the right-hand side should read

$$F'_x\left(\frac{x}{2}\frac{y}{2}\right)$$

38(8) Rearranging this expression gives $(\xi/\eta)=(\phi'_y/\phi'_x)=dx/dy$, which is Jevons's famous formula, the first equation in his 'symbolic statement of the theory'.

38(12) The word 'within' should read 'on'. Edgeworth changed this in his copy.

38(25) The first term should read $\xi F'_x$.

39(10) The first term should read $\xi\phi'_x$.

42(2) 'Below, p. 48' should actually read 'above p. 38'.

44(n. 2) The reference to John Elliot Cairnes is to, *Some Leading Principles of Political Economy Newly Expounded* (1874), in particular to Part II, chapter III pp. 253–87 (Trades Unionism – No. 1).

45(2) Henry Fawcett (1833–84). The reference is to the *Manual of Political Economy* (1863) but the appropriate sections in the 2nd edition (1865) on unproductive labour and consumption are in chapter III (labour as an agent of production), not in chapter IV. Fawcett's discussion of Unions is mainly in chapter IX (Trades Unions and Strikes, pp. 256–76).

47(23) In his copy, Edgeworth added the sentence, 'The sort of knowledge in question may be compared to information about the quantity of the articles other than the price. This fact is exemplified by Railway combinations'.

47(n. 1) Thomas Edward Cliffe Leslie (1827–82), from 1853 Professor of Jurisprudence and Political Economy at Queen's College, Belfast.

47(n. 2) The corresponding reference to the English Translation is § 381 (Part VIII, lesson 41, p. 439) on, 'Cournot's analytical theory of monopoly'.

48(12) There should only be one X here. Edgeworth made the correction in his copy.

49(9) In his copy Edgeworth added, 'and indeed in ordinary factories as to rate of machinery & L'.

50(22) 'Multiety' should read 'multeity'.

51(22) 'Hortative' should read 'hortatory'. Edgeworth corrected this in his copy.

51(n. 1) The reference to 'Data of Ethics' is actually to the first part of Spencer's *Principles of Ethics* (1879). The reference is in chapter IX 'Criticism and Explanations' where Spencer discusses justice and happiness.

51(n. 2) The reference to Dugald Stewart (1753–1829) is perhaps to his *Collected works*, edited by Sir William Hamilton (philosopher, not mathematician) in 11 volumes (1854–60). Stewart was a pupil of Adam Smith and Professor of Moral Philosophy 1785–1810; his pupils included James Mill, McCulloch, Lauderdale, Thomas Chalmers, Henry Brougham, Francis Jeffrey and Francis Horner.

52(1) George Jacob Holyoake (1817–1906) was a tireless proponent of the co-operative movement. In 1842 he was imprisoned for six months for alleged atheism, the last person on trial for this offence in England.

52(n. 1) J. S. Mill's review is 'Thornton on Labour and its Claims' *Fortnightly Review*, May 1869, in which he accepted Thornton's criticism of the wages-fund theory. See The Ashley Edition of Mill's *Principles* (1920, bibliographical note O, pp. 991–3). The review was of Thornton's book, *On Labour: its wrongful claims and Rightful Dues: Its Actual present and Possible Future* (1869).

54(n. 1) This reference is to the section in J. S. Mill's *Principles* on 'Cases in which wages are fixed by custom'.

54(n. 1) This reference to Francis Amasa Walker (1840–97) is to his book *The Wages Question, A Treatise on Wages and the Wages Class* (1876).

55(20) 'Would likely' should read 'would be likely'. Edgeworth corrected this in his copy.

55(n. 2) Against this note in Edgeworth's copy he added, 'Quetelet corrects the Aristotelian mean with his "nombre moyen" but see his page 398 vol. 2 Physique Sociale for principle of conciliation'.

55(n. 2) 'virtue'.

56(20) Pages 56 to 82 contain with some revisions Edgeworth's *Mind* (1879) paper on 'The Hedonical Calculus'. The changes made for the *Psychics* are noted below.

57(n. 1) The reference is to Matthew Arnold (1822–88); see also chapter 2.

57(n. 2) Edgeworth obviously omits the utility function from the integral.

57(n. 2) The last two sentences of this note were added in 1881.

58(2) Edgeworth's reference to 'Mind X' is misleading as *Mind* did not begin publication until 1876, and the X refers to the number not the volume. The reference is to Alfred Barratt (1877).

58(n. 1) The note to chapter XI of *Pessimism* (pp. 326–31) was on 'Differences of Quality in Pleasure'.

59(3) William Thompson (1785–1833), author of *Inquiry into the Principles of the Distribution of Wealth* (1824) and *Labour Rewarded: The Claims of Labour and Capital Conciliated; or How to Secure to Labour the Whole Products of its Exertions* (1827).

59(23) The French socialist Charles Fourier (1772–1837).

59(n. 1) This note was added in 1881.

60(n. 1) Alexander Bain (1818–1903), whose relevant works here are *The Emotions and the Will* (1859) and *The Senses and the Intellect* (1855).

60(n. 2) The last part of this note was of course added in 1881.

61(6) J. A. Venn (1834–1923) author of *The Logic of Chance* (1866), and lecturer in Moral Sciences at Cambridge from 1862.

61(7) 'Skill in measuring'.

61(11) 'leading out', and 'accustoming' respectively.

61(n. 1) This note was added in 1881.

62(1) Buffon's 'Essai d'arithmetique Moral', *Supplement à L'Histoire Naturelle* (Vol. 4, 1777). His full name was Georges-Louis Leclerc, Count of Buffon (1707–88).

62(7) The psychologist Gustav T. Fechner (1801–87), author of *Elements der Psychophysik* (1860).

63(28) The word 'Parallelopiped' should read 'Parallelepiped'.

64(21) The words 'and more pleasure' were added in 1881.

64(25) The word 'educible' should read 'deducible'.

64(n. 1) The footnote was added in 1881.

66(17) 'Well balanced ship'.

66(23) This refers to what is usually called the Brachistochrone problem, posed by Galileo in 1530 and solved by James and John Bernoulli in the 1690s. It concerns the optimal shape of a 'slide' between two points such that a ball runs from the highest to the lowest point in the shortest time.

66(n. 1) The footnote was added in 1881. Edgeworth is probably referring to the note on page 59 of *Mathematical Psychics*.

67(2) The words 'if possible' were added in 1881.

67(19) The last term in the penultimate expression on p. 67 should also contain *c*.

68(18) The words, 'given quantity of a of *means*' should read 'of a given quantity of *means*'.

68(n. 1) On p. 72 of *New and Old Methods of Ethics* Edgeworth quotes Herbert Spencer, Alexander Bain, Adam Smith and his friend James Sully to support his view.

68(n. 2) On p. 77 of *New and Old Methods of Ethics* Edgeworth considers the interdependence between population, wealth and 'felicific progress', at greater length and with even more elusiveness than here.

69(9) This was changed from '$\alpha\beta\lambda$ and $\beta\delta$' to $\alpha\lambda\delta$ in 1881.

69(13) The word 'utilitarian' was added in 1881.

69(n. 1) This footnote was added in 1881.

70(2) Sir Francis Galton (1822–1911): see also chapter 2. The assumption that the capacity of children is normally distributed about the parental capacity is very firmly in the tradition of Galton. Edgeworth avoids the problem of using mid-parent capacity by the assumption of endogamy.

70(3) Adolphe Quételet (1796–1874), Belgian astronomer, meteorologist and social statistician. Quételet popularized the idea of 'L'homme moyen'.

70(n. 1) This footnote was added in 1881.

71(3) The word 'educed' should of course read 'deduced'.

71(28) 'In a humane way'.

72(5) This originally read 'from Utopia to Atopia', but Atopia was deleted in 1881.

72(11) Thomas Doubleday (1790–1870), radical son of a soap manufacturer in Newcastle. The reference is probably to *The True Law of Population shown to be Connected with the Food of the People* (1841) which was an attack on Malthus.

72(n. 1) The reference is to Galton's *Hereditary Genius* (1869).

72(n. 1) Sully (1877, p. 72, n. 1) actually says that, 'he may seek by social sanctions to discourage the multiplication of the confessedly inefficient, if not to encourage by inducements the multiplication of the most efficient'.

73(8) In 1879 this read simply, 'from Atopia'.

75(21) A section headed $\beta\delta$ has been omitted from the 1879 version, but it is not obvious since the sections are ordered α, β, $\alpha\beta$, γ, δ, $\alpha\delta$, $\alpha\gamma\delta$, $\beta\delta$, $\beta\gamma\delta$, $\alpha\beta\gamma\delta$. The missing section is at p. 404 of *Mind* (1879).

76(21) 'arguing plausibly'.

76(22) Edgeworth indicates later (in Appendix III) that he may be referring to Maxwell's Essay on Atoms in *Encyclopaedia Britannica*.

76(29) This is Thomas Hill Green (1836–82). Idealist and Whyte's Professor of moral philosophy at Oxford.

76(30) John Grote, Professor of Moral Philosophy in Cambridge and author of *Examination of the Utilitarian Philosophy* (1870) and *A Treatise on the Moral Ideals* (1876), both edited posthumously by J. S. Mayor. Like Edgeworth, Grote was fond of neologisms.

77(8) 'who has destroyed the citadels of many cities and will destroy yet more, for his strength is very great' (From Illiad 2, 9; of Zeus).

77(13) 'worthy', 'proper'.

78(8) This was changed in 1881 from 'affords' to 'may afford'.

78(12) 'energies'.

78(14) This is a quotation from Tennyson's 'Locksley Hall', but should read, 'Woman is the lesser man, and all thy passions, match'd with mine, Are as moonlight unto sunlight, and as water unto wine'.

78(24) 'more naturally'.

78(n. 2) Edgeworth later said of Edmund Burke (1729–97): 'a rich vein of economic wisdom runs through the whole vast tract of Burke's political writings' and 'he is no bigoted preacher of Laissez-Faire' (Palgrave's *Dictionary*, I, pp. 174–5).

78(n. 3) The famous historian, philosopher and economist David Hume (1711–76).

78(n. 4) This is *Emile, ou de l'éducation* (1762) a partly fictional educational treatise, by Jean-Jacques Rousseau (1712–78).

78(n. 5) This note was of course added in 1881.
79(30) The word 'intuitivist', was changed from 'ituitionist' in 1881.
80(n. 1) This note was added in 1881.
81(16) Robert Owen (1771–1858), the famous 'co-operator'.
82(3) Joseph Butler (1692–1752): see chapter 2.
82(n. 1) This note was added in 1881.
83(4) 'Someone ignorant of geometry'; see also note 5.
84(22) This quotation from the *Saturday Review* has a number of minor errors. For the correct wording see Black (1981, p. 154).
84(n. 1) This reference should be to § 9, not p. 9. The sentence quoted by Edgeworth is incomplete, and Edgeworth omitted a number of commas.
84(n. 2) The sentence from which the quotation is taken begins, 'The algebraic notation, considered as a philosophical language, is perfect in its . . .'. (See p. 707 of the Toronto Edition of Mill's work). Again the quotation is not quite accurate, and Mill does not refer to Comte in this chapter, but mainly to Whewell.
86(24) 'If only I have more good things'.
86(n. 1) Sir George Biddell Airy (1801–92). The book is *On Sound and Atmospheric Vibrations, with the Mathematical Elements of Music* (1868, 1871). Airy was Astronomer Royal, 1835–81.
87(n. 1) This is Jevons's *Principles of Science* (1874).
88(34) 'widely'.
89(18) Bertrand-Thompson should read Bertrand-Thomson.
89(n. 1) 'Activities'.
91(n. 1) The reference should be to Book III (as at p. 84), not to Book IV.
92(26) This is a reference to the mathematician George Wilhelm Strauch (1811–68), although the name is printed as Stranch.
93(26) 'high-mindedness'.
94(8) 'Love itself is to be loved by rule'.
94(23) Hermann Heinrich Gossen (1810–58); see also chapter 4.
94(n. 2) Sir George Howard Darwin (1845–1912), from 1883 Plummer Professor of Astronomy and Experimental Philosophy. Darwin's review of Cairnes' *Leading Principles* in the *Fortnightly Review* (1875) was mainly a defence of Jevons.

94(n. 3) Cairnes actually only accepted that, 'it may be possible to employ . . . mathematical formulae for the purpose of exhibiting economic doctrines *reached by other methods*'. See the *Character and Logical Method of Political Economy* (2nd edition 1875, p. vii).

95(13) This is a quotation from Pope's *Essay on Man*, 2nd Epistle, Argument III. It is repeated on p. 129.

95(24) Francis Anne Kemble (1809–93), from the famous family of actors, went to the United States with her father and married Pierce Butler, a southern planter. She was divorced in 1848 and continued acting under her maiden name.

96(18) This is a reference to Book IV, chapter I (pp. 411–17) 'The Meaning of Utilitarianism' in Sidgwick's *Methods of Ethics*.

96(24) The reference to p. 256 of *Methods of Ethics* is rather odd, as it relates to a section on the duties of affection that arise out of relationships 'voluntarily assumed' especially 'the conjugal relation' (Book III, chapter IV on 'Benevolence').

96(n. 1) These are Cunynghame's 'Notes on Exchange Value' which were privately printed during the 1870s, now lost. See Keynes (1972, pp. 297–307) for a brief sketch.

97(15) 'Speak not of them but look and pass by'. This is a quotation from Dante's *Inferno*, 3, 51.

97(19) 'But he is not so displeased or angered with Hera, for always she has been accustomed to frustrate what he (Zeus) devises'. This is from Illiad, 8. In the previous sentence Here should read Hera.

98(30) 'The art of measurement'.

98(n. 1) Most of p. 9 of the *Theory of Political Economy* is occupied by a quotation from De Morgan concerning measurement.

99(n. 1) This quotation appears on p. 47 of the 5th edition. The two dimensions are concerned with the 'quantity of the commodity' and the 'intensity of the effect produced upon the consumer'.

100(n. 2) On p. 78 of *Theory of Political Economy* Jevons mentions 'urgency of desire', but not in the context of time.

100(n. 3) The reference to 'As You Like It' is to the conversation between Rosamund and Orlando containing the statement by the former that, 'Time travels in divers paces with divers persons. I'll tell you who Time ambles withal, who Time trots withal, who Time gallops withal, and who he stands withal'.

100(n. 3) After this footnote in his own copy Edgeworth added the lines, 'Though in time, second nearly nought, it was eternity to thought'.

102(22) See Sidgwick's *Methods of Ethics*, Book II, 'Egoism'.

102(n. 1) This page of *Data of Ethics* is in chapter IV 'Ways of Judging Conduct'.

103(30) John Austin (1790–1859), the first Professor of Jurisprudence at London University: see also chapter 2.

103(n. 1) Chapter XI is on 'Egoism *versus* Altruism'.

104(38) For consistency x should be printed as X.

105(22) 'not in a genuine demand curve' should read 'not a genuine demand curve'. Edgeworth noted the correction in his copy.

105(31) For Fig. 8 see Whitaker (1975, vol. 2, p. 155).

108(n. 1) Jevons does not actually use the words 'law of increasing toilsomeness of labour', however.

109(n. 2) See Whitaker (1975, Vol. 2, p. 152), where Marshall discusses the use of differential equations to analyse the dynamics of the 'exchange-index'. He says, 'such calculations might afford considerable scope to the ingenuity of those who devise mathematical problems, but they would afford no aid to the Economist'.

109(n. 3) The reference is to the section on the 'law of Indifference'.

110(10) The word 'quantities' should of course read 'equations'.

110(21) The variables x and y should read x' and y'.

110(23) In his copy Edgeworth inserted the phrase, 'a function of course involving a constant'.

110(27) 'Equal to other' should read 'equal to each other'.

113(4) 'A mixed breed'.

114(19) 'may you drown in the deep; one more beautiful has come forth to contend; he will overthrow the untouched victor with much praise'.

115(n. 1) On the anonymous reviewer's discussion of house sales, see chapter 3.

116(20) 'Someone ignorant of geometry'.

116(22) 'will you reprove great Homer?' and 'warts on a fine body'.

117(16) This is a quotation from the Bible: Matthew 6:23.

117(n. 1) Jeremy Bentham (1748–1832). Edgeworth here refers to the earliest collection of Bentham's work, made by J. Bowring in 1838.

117(n. 1) 'Not about the tripod but about the soul'. The tripod probably refers to the prize in an athletic contest.

117(n. 1) Joseph Priestley (1733–1804), theologian and scientist, and member of the 'Lunar Society'; see Schofield (1963).

117(n. 1) The reference to Beccaria is Cesare Bonesanna, Marchese di Beccaria (1738–93). The quotation comes from the preface to *Dei Delitti e delle Pene* (1764); the first English edition of *An Essay on Crimes and Punishment* was in 1767. See also Baumol and Goldfeld (1968, pp. 147–50).

118(n. 1) Edgeworth discusses the meaning of 'the greatest number' on pp. 36–9 of *New and Old Methods of Ethics*.

118(n. 3) This should read 'Pure Theory of Trade'.

119(n. 1) The reference to lesson 15 does not seem appropriate here. The most useful reference is lesson 8 'Utility curves or want curves. The method of maximum utility of commodities' (*Elements*, pp. 115–32).

119(n. 5) On p. 5 of *Leading Principles* Cairnes argues (by analogy with power) that, although 'value' expresses a relation, expressions like the 'sum of values' and 'increase in the aggregate amount of values' may still be used.

119(n. 7) On p. 15 of *Leading Principles* Cairnes says: 'I am wholly unable to conceive how anything amounting to a real explanation can be extracted from the theory we are now considering'.

120(4) 'taken into account, esteemed'.

120(n. 1) This is on p. 100 of the 5th edition of Jevons's *Theory of Political Economy*.

120(n. 2) This is a reference to the section on 'uncertainty of future events' in chapter II of *Theory of Political Economy*.

120(n. 3) The reference to Cairnes, p. 177 would seem to be to the *Leading Principles*, where Cairnes discusses the equality of supply and demand: 'The doctrine of the equality of Demand and Supply as the condition of market price becomes a mere identical proposition. The quantity demanded and the quantity supplied are necessarily equal when the quantity supplied at the market price is only another name for the quantity bought'.

121(7) This quotation from p. 389 of *Leading Principles* should actually read 'as measured in number of days' labour and abstinence'.

121(n. 2) Edgeworth's suggestion that Cairnes contradicted himself on pp. 24–5 and p. 21 of *Leading Principles* is difficult to accept, however.

121(n. 3) Cunyngham should read Cunynghame; see note to p. 96 (n. 1).

121(n. 4) The pages referred to do not clearly suggest that Cairnes viewed the sacrifice of labour as completely 'objective', however.

122(n. 2) On this issue see top of p. 416 of Sidgwick's *Methods of Ethics*.

122(n. 6) This reference to 'above' is mainly to p. 66 of *Mathematical Psychics*.

124(n. 1) This reference to the *Fortnightly Review* is to the paper on 'Economic method'. Sidgwick later (1885) addressed section F of the British Association on, 'The Scope and Method of Economic Science'. The paper is reprinted in R. L. Smyth (ed.) (1962) *Essays in Economic Method 1860–1913*.

124(n. 2) The reference to p. 385 of *Methods of Ethics* is in Book III chapter XII, 'On Philosophical Intuitionism' and does not actually refer to the distribution of happiness.

125(25) In his own copy Edgeworth changed the word 'slight' to 'short'.

126(22) The reference to Sir George Cornewall Lewis (1802–63) is probably to his *Treatise on the Method of Observation and Reasoning in Politics* (1852). Cornewall Lewis was Chancellor of the Exchequer during the Crimean War, and advocated a comprehensive system of low duties; see also chapter 2.

127(11) 'Why should I feel envy, if I can only acquire little'.

127(13) 'The problem is resolved by pacing it out'.

128(14) Helvetius (1715–71), whose *Traité de L'Esprit* (1758) was condemned by the Sorbonne and burnt by the hangman. With reference to Edgeworth's opening sentence of the 'Economical Calculus' (p. 16), it is interesting that Helvetius wrote, 'the principle of interest is for the moral world, what the principle of gravitation is for the physical one' (*de L'Esprit*, Vol. I, div. ii, chapter ii).

129(6) This is from Pope's *Essay on Man*; see note to p. 95(13) above.

130(n. 2) The corresponding page in Whitaker (1975, vol. 2) is p. 132.

131(38) 'monetary pleasure'.

132(n. 2) 'For it is and has been very well said, that what is useful is good and what is harmful is evil'.

134(n. 1) Louis-Antione Fauvelet de Bourrienne (1769–1834) biographer of Napoleon.

134(n. 3) Henry Crompton (1836–1904) a positivist and advocate of Trade Unions. The reference is probably to his *Industrial Conciliation* (1876).

135(n. 1) These references are probably to Cliffe Leslie's 'Political Economy and Sociology', *Fortnightly Review*. (Jan. 1879) and 'On the Philosophical Method of Political Economy' *Hermathena*, no. IV (1876). Both are reprinted in *Essays in Political and Moral Philosophy* (1879).

135(n. 2) Frederic Harrison (1831–1923), a Jurist and English Comtist. Harrison's article, 'Comte and Political Economy', *Fortnightly Review* (May and July 1870) began a controversy with Cairnes. This is discussed in J. K. Ingram (1878). See also Jevons's *Theory of Political Economy* (5th edition, pp. 29–30).

137(16) 'Careful in the hope of indulgence'.

138(n. 2) John Morley, First Viscount Morley of Blackburn (1838–1923); journalist, critic, Liberal politician, biographer of Gladstone and many others, and editor of the *Fortnightly Review*, 1867–82.

139(3) This is from Pope's *Essay on Man*, 2nd Epistle, from line 45. The first line was also used without acknowledgement in Edgeworth (1877, p. 60).

144(5) In his copy Edgeworth changed q/p to p/q.

146(23) This reference to 'the one in the many' is discussed in chapter 3.

147(n. 2) This is a reference to Jevons (1876) 'The future of Political Economy', *Fortnightly Review* (NS, VIII, pp. 617–31).

147(n. 4) This is a reference to p. 176 of *Leading Principles*, where Cairnes actually said, 'every costermonger will tell you this much'.

References

Allen, R. G. D. (1934) A comparison of different definitions of complementary and competitive goods. *Econometrica*, **2**, 168–75.
Annan, N. G. (1955) The intellectual aristocracy. In J. H. Plumb (ed.), *Studies in Social History*. London, 243–87.
Atkinson, A. B. and Stiglitz, J. E. (1980) *Lectures on Public Economics*. London: McGraw-Hill.
Bacharach, M. (1976) *Economics and the Theory of Games*. London: Macmillan.
Bailey, M. J. (1954) Edgeworth's taxation paradox and the nature of demand functions. *Econometrica*, **22**, 72–6.
Ball, N. W. R. (1924) *A Short Account of the History of Mathematics*. London: Macmillan.
Barratt, A. (1869) *Physical Ethics*. London: Macmillan.
Barratt, A. (1877) Ethics and politics, *Mind*, **2**, 425–76.
Baumol, W. J. and Goldfeld, S. M. (1968) *Precursors in Mathematical Economics: An Anthology*. London School of Economics Reprints of Scarce Works in Political Economy, no. 19.
Bhagwati, J. (1958) Immiserizing growth: a geometric note. *Review of Economic Studies*, **25**, 201–5.
Bickerdike, C. F. (1906) The theory of incipient taxes. *Economic Journal*, **16**, 529–35.
Black, R. D. C. (1962) Jevons and the economists of his time. *Manchester School*, **30**, 203–21.
Black, R. D. C. (1970) *Jevons's Theory of Political Economy*. London: Penguin.
Black, R. D. C. (ed.) (1977a) *Papers and Correspondence of William Stanley Jevons*, Vol. III, *Correspondence 1863–1872*. London: Macmillan, for the Royal Economic Society.
Black, R. D. C. (ed.) (1977b) *Papers and Correspondence of William Stanley Jevons*, Vol. IV, *Correspondence 1873–1878*. London: Macmillan, for the Royal Economic Society.

Black, R. D. C. (ed.) (1977c) *Papers and Correspondence of William Stanley Jevons*, Vol. V, *Correspondence 1879–1882*. London: Macmillan, for the Royal Economic Society.

Black, R. D. C. (ed.) (1981) *Papers and Correspondence of William Stanley Jevons*, Vol. VII, *Papers on Political Economy*. London: Macmillan, for the Royal Economic Society.

Black, R. D. C. and Könekamp, R. (1972) *Papers and Correspondence of William Stanley Jevons*, Vol. I, *Biography and Personal Journal*. London: Macmillan, for the Royal Economic Society.

Blaug, M. (1968) *Economic Theory in Retrospect*. 2nd edn, London: Heinemann.

Blum, W. J. and Kalven, K. (1953) *The Uneasy Case for Progressive Taxation*. Chicago: Chicago University Press.

Bonar, J. (1926) Memories of F. Y. Edgeworth. *Economic Journal*, **37**, 647–53.

Bowley, A. L. (1924) *The Mathematical Groundwork of Economics*. Oxford: Clarendon Press.

Bowley, A. L. (1928) *Edgeworth's Contribution to Mathematical Statistics*. London: Royal Statistical Society.

Bowley, A. L. (1934) Francis Ysidro Edgeworth. *Econometrica*, **1**, 113–24.

Bradley, F. H. (1876) *Ethical Studies*. Oxford: Oxford University Press.

Bradley, F. H. (1877) Mr. Sidgwick's hedonism. *Mind*. Rep. (1925) in *Collected Essays*, Oxford: Oxford University Press.

Burrows, J. H. (1978) The teaching of economics in the early days of the university extension movement in London 1876–1902. *History of Economic Thought Newsletter*, **20**, 8–14.

Butler, J. H. and Butler, H. E. (1927) *The Black Book of Edgeworthtown and other Edgeworth Memories 1585–1817*. London: Faber and Gwyer.

Butler, M. S. (1972) *Maria Edgeworth; A Literary Biography*. Oxford: Oxford University Press.

Cairnes, J. E. (1872) New theories of political economy. *Fortnightly Review*, **11**, 72–7.

Cantillon, R. (1755) *Essai sur la Nature du Commerce en Général*, tr. (1931) H. Higgs (ed.), London: Macmillan, for the Royal Economic Society.

Chipman, J. (1977) An empirical implication of Auspitz–Lieben–Edgeworth–Pareto complementarity. *Journal of Economic Theory*, **14**, 228–31.

Clark, I. C. (1949) *Maria Edgeworth: Her Family and Friends*. London: Hutchinson.

Clifford, W. K. (1879) *Lectures and Essays*, L. Stephen and F. Pollock (eds), London: Macmillan.

Clifford, W. K. (1882) *Mathematical Papers*, R. Tucker (ed.). London: Macmillan.

Coats, A. W. (1961) Alfred Marshall and Richard T. Ely: some unpublished letters. *Economica*, **28**, 191–4.

Coats, A. W. (1967) Sociological aspects of British economic thought 1880–1930. *Journal of Political Economy*, **75**, 706–29.

Coats, A. W. (1968) The origins and early development of the Royal Economic Society. *Economic Journal*, **78**, 349–71.

Collard, D. (1975) Edgeworth's propositions on altruism. *Economic Journal*, **85**, 355–60.

Collard, D. (1978) *Altruism and Economy*. Oxford: Martin Robertson.

Colvin, C. (1972) *Maria Edgeworth, Letters from England 1813–1844*. Oxford: Oxford University Press.

Colvin, C. (1979) *Maria Edgeworth in France and Switzerland*. Oxford: Oxford University Press.

Cournot, A. A. (1838) *Researches into the Mathematical Principles of the Theory of Wealth*, tr. (1927) N. T. Bacon; I. Fisher, (ed.), London: Stechert–Hafner.

Creedy, J. (1979) Edgeworth's contribution to the theory of exchange. *Scottish Journal of Political Economy*, **26**, 163–81.

Creedy, J. (1980a) Some recent interpretations of Mathematical Psychics. *History of Political Economy*, **12**, 267–76.

Creedy, J. (1980b) The early use of Lagrange multipliers in economics. *Economic Journal*, **90**, 371–6.

Creedy, J. (1981) F. Y. Edgeworth 1845–1926. In D. P. O'Brien and J. R. Presley (eds), In D. P. O'Brien and J. R. Presley (eds), *Pioneers of Modern Economics In Britain*. London: Macmillan, 72–104.

Creedy, J. (1983) F. Y. Edgeworth's mathematical training. *Journal of the Royal Statistical Society*, A, **146**, 158–62.

Creedy, J. (1984a) Public finance. In J. Creedy and D. P. O'Brien (eds), In J. Creedy and D. P. O'Brien (eds), *Economic Analysis in Historical Perspective*. London: Butterworth, 84–116.

Creedy, J. (1984b) Edgeworth: arbitration and utilitarianism. *History of Political Economy*, **16**, 609–18.

Deaton, A. S. (1974) A reconsideration of the empirical implications of additive preferences. *Economic Journal*, **84**, 338–48.

Dooley, P. C. (1983) Consumer's surplus: Marshall and his critics. *Canadian Journal of Economics*, **16**, 26–38.

Doresamienger, M. R. (1929) Some recent developments in the mathematical theory of taxation due to Edgeworth. *Indian Journal of Economics*, **10**, 317–31.

Dwyer, G. P. and Lindsay, C. M. (1984) Robert Giffen and the Irish potato. *American Economic Review*, **63**, 188–92.

Edgeworth, F. Y. (1876) Mr. Matthew Arnold on Bishop Butler's doctrine of self love. *Mind*, **1**, 570–1.

Edgeworth, F. Y. (1877) *New and Old Methods of Ethics: or 'Physical Ethics' and 'Methods of Ethics'*. Oxford: Parker.

Edgeworth, F. Y. (1879) The hedonical calculus. *Mind*, **4**, 394–408.

Edgeworth, F. Y. (1881) *Mathematical Psychics: An Essay on the Application of Mathematics to the Moral Sciences*. London: Kegan Paul.

Edgeworth, F. Y. (1882) Mr. Leslie Stephen on utilitarianism. *Mind*, **7**, 446–7.

Edgeworth, F. Y. (1887) *Metretike, or the Method of Measuring Probability and Utility*. London: Temple.

Edgeworth, F. Y. (1909) Review of free trade in being. *Economic Journal*, **19**, 104–5.

Edgeworth, F. Y. (1925) *Papers Relating to Political Economy*. 3 vols. London: Macmillan, for the Royal Economic Society.

Edgeworth, M. (1820) *Memories of Richard Lovell Edgeworth Esq., Begun by Himself and Concluded by his Daughter, Maria Edgeworth*, 2 vols. London: Hunter.

Ekelund, R. B. and Herbert, R. F. (1983) *A History of Economic Theory and Method*. New York: McGraw-Hill.

Evans, G. C. (1930) *A Mathematical Introduction to Economics*.

Fagan, E. D. (1938) Recent and contemporary theories of progressive taxation. *Journal of Political Economy*, **46**, 457–98.

Farebrother, R. W. (1983) A genealogy of Charles Darwin, Francis Galton and Francis Ysidro Edgeworth. University of Manchester (mimeo).

Farrell, M. J. (1970) Edgeworth's bounds for oligopoly prices. *Economica*, **49**, 341–61.

Ferguson, C. E. (1958) Modified Edgeworth phenomena and the nature of related commodities. In R. W. Pfouts (ed.), *Essays in Economics and Econometrics*. Chapel Hill: University of North Carolina Press, 178–87.

Fisher, I. (1892) *Mathematical Investigations in the Theory of Value and Prices*. Rep. 1925. New Haven: Yale University Press.

Fisher, I. (1925) Edgeworth's papers relating to Political Economy. *Quarterly Journal of Economics*, **40**, 167–71.

Fisher, I. (1927) A statistical method for measuring marginal utility and testing the justice of a progressive income tax. In J. H. Hollander (ed.), *Economic Essays in honour of John Bates Clark*. New York: American Economic Association, 157–93.

Fisher, I. N. (1956) *My Father Irving Fisher*. New York: Comet Press.

Forrest, D. W. (1974) *Francis Galton; the Life and Work of a Victorian Genius*. London: Elek.

Friedman, R. B. (1969) An introduction to Mill's theory of authority. In J. B. Schneewind (ed.), *Mill: A Collection of Critical Essays*. London: Macmillan, 479–525.

Friendly, A. (1977) *Beaufort of the Admiralty, the Life of Sir Francis Beaufort 1774–1857*. London: Hutchinson.

Galton, F. (1908) *Memories of my life*. London: Methuen.

Garver, R. (1933) The Edgeworth taxation phenomenon. *Econometrica*, **1**, 402–7.

Graham, F. (1923) The theory of international values re-examined. *Quarterly Journal of Economics*, **37**, 54–86.

Gramm, W. P. (1970) Giffen's paradox and the Marshallian demand curve. *Manchester School*, **38**, 55–61.

ORDER NUMBER
PO NYAATP08

BOOK NUMBER
9549726

BAY NUMBER
6093-9

AUTHOR	Creedy, John
TITLE	Edgeworth and the Development of

Graves, A. P. (1931) *To Return to All That*. London: Cape.
Graves, R. (1960) *Goodbye to All That*, 2nd edn. London: Penguin.
Graves, R. P. (1882) *Life of William Rowan Hamilton*. London: Longmans, Green.
Groenewegen, P. D. (1970) A reappraisal of Turgot's theory of value, exchange and price determination. *History of Political Economy*, **2**, 177–96.
Halsey, A. H. (ed.) (1976) *Traditions of Social Policy: Essays in Honour of Violet Butler*. Oxford: Basil Blackwell.
Harsanyi, J. C. (1953) Cardinal utility in welfare economics and in the theory of risk taking. *Journal of Political Economy*, **61**, 434–5.
Harsanyi, J. C. (1955) Cardinal welfare, individualistic ethics, and interpersonal comparisons of utility. *Journal of Political Economy*, **63**, 309–21.
Hemming, G. W. (1852) *A Just Income Tax: How Possible*. London: Chapman.
Herford, C. H. (1931) *Philip Henry Wicksteed: His Life and Work*. London: Dent.
Hicks, J. R. (1930) Edgeworth, Marshall and the indeterminateness of wages. *Economic Journal*, **40**, 215–31.
Hicks, J. R. (1939) *Value and Capital*. Oxford: Clarendon Press.
Hicks, J. R. and Allen, R. G. D. (1934) A reconsideration of the theory of value. *Economica*, **14**, 52–76, 196–219.
Higgs, H. (ed.) (1925) *Palgrave's Dictionary of Political Economy*. London: Macmillan.
Hildebrand, W. and Kirman, A. (1976) *General Equilibrium Analysis*. Amsterdam: North Holland.
Hobson, J. A. (1938) *Confessions of an Economic Heretic*. London: Allen and Unwin.
Hotelling, H. (1932) Edgeworth's taxation paradox and the nature of demand and supply functions. *Journal of Political Economy*, **40**, 577–616.
Hotelling, H. (1933) Note on Edgeworth's taxation phenomenon and Professor Garver's additional condition on demand functions. *Econometrica*, **1**, 408–9.
Hotelling, H. (1938) The general welfare in relation to problems of taxation and of railway and utility rates. *Econometrica*, **7**, 151–5.
Hotelling, H. (1939) The work of Henry Schultz. *Econometrica*, **7**, 97–103.
Hutchison, T. W. (1953) *A Review of Economic Doctrines 1870–1929*. Oxford: Clarendon Press.
Hutchison, T. W. (1955) Insularity and cosmopolitanism in economic ideas 1870–1914. *American Economic Association. Papers and Proceedings*, **45**, 1–16.
Hutchison, T. W. (1981) *The Politics and Philosophy of Economics*. Oxford: Basil Blackwell.
Ingram, J. K. (1878) The present position and prospects of political economy. Rep. (1962) in R. L. Smyth (ed.), *Essays in Economic Method*. London: Duckworth, 41–72.

Ingram, J. K. (1893) *History of Political Economy*. Edinburgh: Black.
Jaffé, W. (1964) New light on an old quarrel. Rep. in W. J. Baumol and S. M. Goldfeld (eds), *Precursors in Mathematical Economics*. London: London School of Economics, 309–12.
Jaffé, W. (1974a) Edgeworth's contract curve: a propadeutic essay in clarification. *History of Political Economy*, **6**, 343–59.
Jaffé, W. (1974b) Edgeworth's contract curve: two figures in its proto-history: Aristotle and Gossen. *History of Political Economy*, **6**, 381–404.
Jaffé, W. (1977) The birth of Walras's Elements. *History of Political Economy*, **9**, 198–213.
Jenkin, F. (1871) On the principles which regulate the incidence of taxes. *Proceedings of the Royal Society of Edinburgh*. Rep. in R. A. Musgrave and C. S. Shoup (eds), *Readings in the Economics of Taxation*. London: Allen and Unwin, 227–39.
Jenkin, F. (1931) *The Graphic Representation of the Laws of Supply and Demand, and other Essays on Political Economy*. L.S.E. Reprints of Scarce Tracts, No. 9. London: Longmans, Green.
Jevons, H. A. (ed.) (1886) *Letters and Journal of W. Stanley Jevons*. London: Macmillan.
Jevons, W. S. (1881) Review of *Mathematical Psychics*. *Mind*, **6**, 581–3.
Jevons, W. S. (1957) *The Theory of Political Economy*, 5th edn: H. S. Jevons (ed.). New York: Augustus Kelly.
Jha, N. (1973) *The Age of Marshall: Aspects of British Economic Thought 1890–1915*, 2nd edn. London: Cass.
Johnson, E. S. and Johnson, H. (1978) *The Shadow of Keynes*. Oxford: Basil Blackwell.
Johnson, H. G. (1953) Optimum tariffs and retaliation. *Review of Economic Studies*, **21**, 142–53.
Johnson, W. E. (1913) The pure theory of utility curves. *Economic Journal*, **23**, 483–513.
Kendall, M. G. (1970) F. Y. Edgeworth. In E. S. Pearson and M. G. Kendall (eds), *Studies in the History of Statistics and Probability*. London: Griffin, 257–63.
Keynes, M. J. (1936) *The General Theory of Employment, Interest and Money*. London: Macmillan.
Keynes, J. M. (1972) *Essays in Biography*. Vol. X of the *Collected Writings* of Keynes. London: Macmillan, for the Royal Economic Society.
Launhardt, W. (1885) *Mathematische Begründung der Volkswirtschafts Lehre*. Leipzig: Engelmann.
Lawless, E. (1904) *Maria Edgeworth*. London: Macmillan.
Leontief, W. W. (1933) The use of indifference curves in the analysis of foreign trade. *Quarterly Journal of Economics*, **47**, 493–503.
Lerner, A. P. (1936) The symmetry of import and export taxes. *Economica*, **3**, 308–13.
Lerner, A. P. (1947) *The Economics of Control*. New York: Macmillan.

Mackenzie, N. and Mackenzie, J. (eds) (1983) *The Diary of Beatrice Webb, Vol. I, 1873–1892. Glitter Around the Darkness Within*. London: Virago, in association with the London School of Economics.

Marshall, A. (1879) *The Pure Theory of Foreign Trade. The Pure Theory of Domestic Values*. In J. K. Whitaker (ed.), *The Early Economic Writings of Alfred Marshall 1867–1980*. London: Macmillan, for the Royal Economic Society.

Marshall, A. (1881) Review of *Mathematical Psychics*. Rep. (1975) in J. K. Whitaker (ed.), *The Early Economic Writings of Alfred Marshall 1867–1870*. London: Macmillan, for the Royal Economic Society, 265–7.

Marshall, A. (1890) *Principles of Economics*. 9th (variorum) edn (1961) C. W. Guillebaud (ed.), 2 vols. London: Macmillan.

Marshall, A. (1919) *Industry and Trade*. London: Macmillan.

Marshall, A. and Marshall, M. P. (1879) *Economics of Industry*. London: Macmillan.

Meade, J. E. (1952) *A Geometry of International Trade*. London: Allen and Unwin.

Meek, R. L. (ed.) (1973) *Precursors of Adam Smith 1750–1775*. London: Dent.

Mill, J. S. (1848) *Principles of Political Economy*. Rep. (1920) with editorial material by W. J. Ashley. London: Longmans, Green.

Mirrlees, J. A. (1971) An exploration in the theory of optimal income taxation. *Review of Economic Studies*, **38**, 175–208.

Mirrlees, J. A. (1982) The economic uses of utilitarianism. In A. K. Sen and B. Williams (eds), *Utilitarianism and Beyond*. Cambridge: Cambridge University Press, 63–84.

Morgenstern, O. (1941) Professor Hicks on value and capital. *Journal of Political Economy*, **49**, 368–77.

Musgrave, R. A. (1959) *The Theory of Public Finance*. New York: McGraw Hill.

Nichol, A. J. (1935) Edgeworth's theory of duopoly price. *Economic Journal*, **45**, 51–66.

O'Brien, D. P., Darnell, A. C. and Peters, J. (1983) A statistical technique for the investigation of authorship puzzles. *University of Durham Working Papers in Economics*, No. 59.

Pantaleoni, M. (1889) *Pure Economics*, tr. (1898) T. Boston Bruce. London: Macmillan.

Pantaleoni, M. (1923) Obituary of V. Pareto. *Economic Journal*, **33**, 582–90.

Pattanaik, P. K. (1968) Risk, impersonality and the social welfare function. *Journal of Political Economy*, **76**, 1152–69.

Phelps, E. S. (ed.) (1973) *Economic Justice*. London: Penguin.

Phelps Brown, E. H. (1980) Sir Roy Harrod: a biographical memoir. *Economic Journal*, **90**, 1–33.

Pierson, N. G. (1902) *Principles of Economics*, tr. A. A. Wotzel. London: Macmillan.
Pigou, A. C. (1908) *Protective and Preferential Import Duties*. London: Macmillan.
Pigou, A. C. (1910) A method of determining the numerical value of elasticities of demand. *Economic Journal*, **20**, 636–40.
Pigou, A. C. (1925a) Professor Edgeworth's collected papers. *Economic Journal*, **25**, 177–85.
Pigou, A. C. (ed) (1925b) *Memorials of Alfred Marshall 1842–1924*. London: Macmillan.
Pigou, A. C. (1947) *A Study in Public Finance*. London: Macmillan.
Pigou, A. C. (1953) *Alfred Marshall and Current Thought*. London: Macmillan.
Pigou, A. C. and Robertson, D. H. (1931) *Economic Essays and Addresses*. London: King.
Pratt, J. W. (1976) F. Y. Edgeworth and R. A. Fisher on the efficiency of maximum likelihood estimation. *Annals of Statistics*, **4**, 501–14.
Prest, A. R. (1979) The structure and reform of direct taxation. *Economic Journal*, **89**, 243–60.
Price, L. L. (1926) Obituary of Edgeworth. *Journal of the Royal Statistical Society*, **89**, 371–7.
Price, L. L. (1946) Memoirs and Notes on British Economists 1881–1946. MSS, Brotherton Library, University of Leeds.
Rawls, J. (1967) Distributive justice. In P. Laslett and W. G. Runciman (eds), *Philosophy, Politics and Society*. Oxford: Basil Blackwell, 58–82.
Rawls, J. (1971) *A Theory of Justice*. Oxford: Oxford University Press.
Robbins, L. (1970) *Evolution of Modern Economic Theory*. London: Macmillan.
Robertson, D. H. (1931) *Economic Fragments*. London: King.
Robertson, D. H. (1952) *Utility and All That*. London: George Allen and Unwin.
Samuelson, P. A. (1947) *Foundations of Economic Analysis*. Cambridge, MA: Harvard University Press.
Samuelson, P. A. (1974) Complementarity: an essay on the 40th anniversary of the Hicks–Allen revolution in demand theory. *Journal of Economic Literature*, **12**, 1255–89.
Schneewind, J. B. (1977) *Sidgwick's Ethics and Victorian Moral Philosophy*. Oxford: Oxford University Press.
Schofield, R. E. (1963) *The Lunar Society of Birmingham*. Oxford: Clarendon Press.
Schotter, A. and Schwodiauer, G. (1980) Economics and game theory: a survey. *Journal of Economic Literature*, **18**, 479–527.
Schultz, H. (1933) Interrelations of demand. *Journal of Political Economy*, **41**, 468–512.
Schultz, H. (1938) *The Theory and Measurement of Demand*. Chicago: University of Chicago Press.

Schumpeter, J. A. (1952) *Ten Great Economists*. London: Allen and Unwin.

Schumpeter, J. A. (1954) *History of Economic Analysis*. London: Allen and Unwin.

Seligman, E. R. A. (1921) *Shifting and the Incidence of Taxation*. New York: Macmillan.

Sen, A. (1973) *On Economic Inequality*. Oxford: Clarendon Press.

Shehab, F. (1953) *Progressive Taxation: A Study in the Development of the Progressive Principle in the British Public Tax*. Oxford: Oxford University Press.

Shubik, M. (1959) Edgcworth market games. In R. D. Luce and A. W. Tucker (eds), *Contributions to the Theory of Games, Vol. 4*. Princeton, NJ: Princeton University Press, 267–78.

Sidgwick, A. and Sidgwick, E. M. (1906) *Henry Sidgwick: A Memoir*. London: Macmillan.

Sidgwick, H. (1874) *The Methods of Ethics*. London: Macmillan.

Spencer, H. (1879) *The Principles of Ethics*. New York: Appleton. Reprinted 1978. Indianapolis: Liberty Classics.

Stigler, G. J. (1941) *Production and Distribution Theories*. New York: Macmillan.

Stigler, G. J. (1965) *Essays in the History of Economics*. Chicago: Chicago University Press.

Stigler, S. M. (1978) Francis Ysidro Edgeworth, Statistician. *Journal of the Royal Statistical Society*, A, **141**, 287–322.

Streissler, E. (1972) To what extent was the Austrian school marginalist? In R. D. C. Black, A. W. Coats and C. D. W. Goodwin (eds), *The Marginal Revolution in Economics*. Durham: Duke University Press, 160–75.

Sully, J. (1877) *Pessimism: A History and a Criticism*. London: Fisher Unwin.

Sully, J. (1918) *My Life and Friends*. London: Fisher Unwin.

Tait, A. (1867) *Elementary Treatise on Quaternions*. London: Macmillan.

Tarascio, V. J. (1972) A correction: on the genealogy of the so-called Edgeworth–Bowley diagram. *Western Economic Journal*, **10**, 193–7.

Thornton, W. T. (1869) *On Labour: Its Wrongful Claims and Rightful Dues, Its Actual Present and Possible Future*. London.

Vickrey, W. S. (1958) Can excises lower prices? In R. W. Pfouts (ed.), *Essays in Economics and Econometrics*. Chapel Hill: University of North Carolina Press, 165–77.

Vickrey, W. S. (1960) Utility, strategy and social decision rules. *Quarterly Journal of Economics*, **74**, 507–35.

Viner, J. (1958) *The Long View and the Short*. Glencoe: Free Press.

Viner, J. (1964) *Studies in the Theory of International Trade*. London: Allen and Unwin.

Walker, D. A. (1973) Edgeworth's theory of recontract. *Economic Journal*, **83**, 138–49.

Walras, L. (1874) *Elements of Pure Economics*, tr. (1954) W. Jaffé. London: Allen and Unwin.

Webb, S. and Webb, B. (1919) *Industrial Democracy*. London: Longman.

Weintraub, E. R. (1977) The microfoundations of macroeconomics: a critical survey. *Journal of Economic Literature*, **14**, 1–23.

Whitaker, J. K. (ed.) (1975) *The Early Economic Writings of Alfred Marshall 1867–1890*. London: Macmillan.

Whitaker, J. K. (1977) Some neglected aspects of Alfred Marshall's economic and social thought. *History of Political Economy*, **9**, 162–97.

Wicksell, K. (1893) *Value, Capital and Rent*, tr. (1954) S. H. Frowein. London: Allen and Unwin.

Wicksell, K. (1901) *Lectures on Political Economy*, Vol. I, tr. (1934) E. Classen. London: Routledge.

Wicksell, K. (1958) *Selected Papers on Economic Theory*, E. Lindahl (ed.). London: George Allen and Unwin.

Wicksteed, P. H. (1894) *The Coordination of the Laws of Distribution*. London: Macmillan.

Wold, H. and Jureen, L. (1953) *Demand Analysis*. New York: Wiley.

Young, A. B. (1927) *Economic Problems Old and New*. New York: Houghton Mifflin.

Zeuthen, F. (1930) *Problems of Monopoly and Economic Warfare*. London: Routledge.

Index

Index by Joyce Kerr